The Master Musicians

New Series Edited by Eric Blom, C.B.E., D.Litt.

TCHAIKOVSKY

The Master Musicians

TCHAIKOVSKY

by

EDWIN EVANS

ML
410
C4E8
1949

Illustrated

London   *J. M. Dent and Sons Ltd*

New York   *Farrar, Straus and Cudahy Inc.*

To
B. N.

PREFACE

I T is nearly forty years since I wrote this book. That my views should have remained unchanged was scarcely to be expected. At first it was almost as a stranger that I approached the task of revision, and there were moments when the enthusiasm of my younger self seemed exaggerated, until I recalled that in those days the need of proselytism still existed, as only a handful of Tchaikovsky's works could be described as familiar. Apart from that I found the ardour of my young predecessor, if occasionally indiscreet, not unprepossessing, and after reflection decided not to moderate it, especially as to have done so would have involved almost writing the book anew. For the latter reason I have also been more indulgent to his literary style than I would be to that of the man he is today, who, I hope, has become more proficient. I trust that the reader will be equally indulgent.

When writing the book my chief guide was Paul Juon's complete German translation of Modest Tchaikovsky's *Life and Letters* of his brother. (Rosa Newmarch's excellent English translation, in abridged form, appeared the same year as my original volume, but was not available while I was engaged upon it.) In that version the dates appeared as 'Old Style,' and I retained them, chiefly because a profusion of double dates made the page look cumbersome. In this edition, however, all dates have been turned into 'New Style' (twelve days ahead of the nineteenthcentury Russian calendar), Soviet Russia having adopted the Gregorian calendar in 1917.

E. E.

March 1943.

CONTENTS

CHAP.   PAGE
    I. EARLY YEARS 1
   II. REMOVAL TO MOSCOW 14
  III. GROWING REPUTATION 21
  IV. FULL MATURITY 33
   V. THE LAST YEARS 43
  VI. THE MAN AND HIS MUSIC 53
 VII. THE OPERAS 57
VIII. INCIDENTAL MUSIC AND BALLETS . . . 93
  IX. THE SYMPHONIES 104
   X. OTHER ORCHESTRAL WORKS 128
  XI. CHAMBER MUSIC 150
 XII. CONCERTOS 159
XIII. PIANO MUSIC AND SONGS 169
XIV. CONCLUSION 179

APPENDICES

A. CALENDAR 189
B. CATALOGUE OF WORKS 211
C. PERSONALIA 221
D. BIBLIOGRAPHY 228

INDEX 229

ILLUSTRATIONS

PORTRAIT OF TCHAIKOVSKY . . . . *Frontispiece*

PORTRAIT OF ALEXANDRA ANDREIEVNA TCHAI-
   KOVSKY IN 1848 . . . . . . *facing page* 3

ILYA PETROVITCH TCHAIKOVSKY IN 1860 . ,, ,, 10

THE COMPOSER'S BIRTHPLACE AT VOTKINSK . ,, ,, 20

TCHAIKOVSKY IN 1863 . . . . ,, ,, 25

TCHAIKOVSKY DURING THE LAST YEARS OF HIS
   LIFE (*Copyright of E. Hatzfeld*) . . . ,, ,, 52

FACSIMILE OF A LETTER TO FRANCESCO BERGER ,, ,, 129

FACSIMILE OF THE COMPOSER'S MANUSCRIPT . ,, ,, 140

CHAPTER I

EARLY YEARS

It is possible that the family from which Tchaikovsky sprang may have had a Polish origin, but in the absence of any documentary evidence, the composer himself insisted with great firmness on his purely Russian nationality. His great-grandfather, Feodor Afanassievich Tchaikovsky, was an officer of Cossacks in the reign of Peter the Great, and fought in the Battle of Poltava. His grandfather, Peter Feodorovich Tchaikovsky, was a nobleman in the government of Kazan.

The youngest of the latter's sons, Ilya Petrovich, was born in 1795. He was educated as a mining engineer, and passed his examinations in 1817, receiving a Government appointment in August the same year. Although the comparative success he achieved in his profession affords proof that he had acquired some proficiency in it, he does not appear to have been otherwise a man of great general culture. He had a certain liking for music, which, however, had not tempted him to acquire any knowledge of the art, and if hereditary influences play any part whatever in the genius of Tchaikovsky, they must be traced on the mother's side. Ilya Petrovich was from all accounts one of those genial and sunny temperaments which are almost destined to be taken advantage of. His confidence in his fellow men had no limits, and the material reverses to which it led could not embitter his character, which was that of a thoroughly kind-hearted and straightforward gentleman. His first wife was Maria Karlovna Keiser, whom he married 23rd September 1827, and by whom he had a daughter, Zinaida; she died soon after, and he married, on 13th October 1833, Alexandra Andreievna Assière. She belonged to a French family which had emigrated at the time of the Revolution, her father, André Assière, having settled in Russia when young. Without being exactly beautiful, Alexandra Andreievna is described as a lady of graceful and dignified presence, with singularly well-shaped hands. She was an accomplished linguist, played the piano and sang the songs of the day in an agreeable but not very powerful voice. Her brother Michael and her sister Catherine were also musically inclined, the latter being well known in St. Petersburg society as a cultured amateur vocalist.

In 1837 Ilya Petrovich obtained a lucrative appointment at Votkinsk in the government of Vyatka. He was entrusted with the management of an important mine, and this position rendered him one of the most prominent men of the district. He lived in the style of the great landowners, had an imposing house and a large staff of servants, in addition to which the Government placed a company of one hundred Cossacks under his orders. Here were born three of his sons—Nicholas (21st May 1838), Peter (7th May 1840),[1] Hippolytus (22nd April 1844), and one daughter, Alexandra (9th January 1843). The family in those days consisted further of an old aunt of Ilya Petrovich and two of his nieces, one of whom, Lydia Vladimirovna, had the misfortune to lose her mother about this time.

The task of giving the children their first instruction fell to a young governess, Fanny Durbach. When she was engaged in November 1844 for his brother Nicholas and his cousin

[1] 7th May, N.S.

ALEXANDRA ANDREIEVNA TCHAIKOVSKY IN 1848
The composer's mother

Lydia, Peter was only four and a half years old, and it was not intended to give him his first lessons until later; but he was so upset, and begged so pitifully to be allowed to join the others, that no further objections were made. He appears to have been an affectionate and sensitive child, and any reproaches or fault-finding had such an exaggerated effect upon him, that it would not have been surprising if he had been spoilt; but Mlle Durbach, although quite captivated by her pupil, was too good a teacher to allow any preference to appear. He studied with great facility, and as the work expected of him consequently did not absorb all the time at his disposal, he soon occupied himself with the piano.

Votkinsk was not a musical town. There were few opportunities for hearing any music, and Peter Ilyich himself was wont to say that the first impetus was given him, not by any human agency, but by a large musical box which his father brought home from St. Petersburg. His great delight was to play by ear on the piano the repertory of the instrument. His favourite piece at this time was an aria from *Don Giovanni,* so that the great admiration he had all his life for Mozart may be said to have manifested itself at a very early age. When he was about six years old, his parents judged the leanings he displayed towards music sufficiently pronounced for him to be taught the piano, and engaged Marie Markovna Paltchikov to teach him.

In 1848 Ilya Petrovich heard of a valuable appointment in Moscow, and he resigned his position at Votkinsk. When, however, he arrived at Moscow towards the end of the year he found that a friend, to whom he had indiscreetly spoken about his prospects, had obtained the very post for which he had journeyed thither. He then migrated to St. Petersburg in search of employment, but failing to find any of a congenial nature in the capital, he was driven to accept the management of the Yakovlev mines in Alapayev in 1849. The life there was much the same as it had been at Votkinsk, except that the appointment, being a private one, did not carry the same prestige as that which he had enjoyed under Government.

Almost immediately on the arrival of the family at St. Petersburg Peter Ilyich was sent to a boarding-school, and it is reported that after the tender care with which the perhaps over-sensitive boy had hitherto been treated the more drastic methods of his school teachers had the effect of making him low-spirited. At the same time he was learning to play the piano with Philipov, and the amount of mental work occasioned by these various studies, coupled with the excitement of frequent visits to the theatre and to the concert room, caused an intellectual and physical strain which brought him to a low state of health. It is not surprising, therefore, to hear that when he and his brother Nicholas were attacked by their first childish complaint, measles, it became a much more serious matter for Peter than for the other patient. The course of the disease was further complicated by nervous attacks, alarming in one so young. This illness left him to some extent changed for the worse. His mother wrote about this time that he was unrecognizable, and had become lazy and troublesome. Some improvement was temporarily effected by the engagement of a new governess, who appears to have wielded a beneficial influence over him; but except in music, to which he was always devoted, he made little progress until he was taken back to St. Petersburg in August 1850 to become a law student.

A few months before, the family had been increased by the twin brothers Anatol and Modest, the latter of whom was destined to become the composer's biographer.

It had originally been the intention of Tchaikovsky's parents to place Peter in the School of Mines, which his elder brother had already attended, but presumably owing to the recommendation of M. A. Vacker, an old friend of Ilya Petrovich, it was decided to send him to the School of Jurisprudence. As the boy had not yet reached the requisite age to attend the regular classes, he was put in the preparatory division. His mother remained in St. Petersburg until about the middle of October, and her departure for Alapayev caused him the greatest despair. He so far lost control of himself that he had to be held back while she got into the carriage, and the moment he was free he ran after it and tried to hold the wheels. This separation from his family and the consequent homesickness had a depressing effect upon him, which lasted until they were reunited in St. Petersburg two years later. Ilya Petrovich's savings, added to the pension to which he was entitled as a former State official, enabled him to retire from active pursuits and give himself up to the quiet and uneventful mode of living which suited him best. The family history about this period is devoid of any interesting incidents. Peter left the preparatory section of the school behind him and began the upward journey through the classes, with perhaps more than the average measure of success, but not rapidly enough to enable one to describe him as a brilliant scholar. The anecdotes which are extant are too irrelevant to find their place in a book of such modest dimensions as the present volume.

In June 1854 a great misfortune overtook the family. Alexandra Andreievna succumbed to an attack of cholera; and Ilya Petrovich almost shared the same fate. It is safe to say that Peter never entirely recovered from the shock. His affection for his mother had been something more than the ordinary filial devotion: it was a veritable passion, and her early demise, during the most impressionable years of his life, was probably the primary cause of the morbid depression and pessimistic vein which overshadows so much of his work. Those who ascribe to his last work, the 'Pathetic' Symphony, an autobiographical significance point to the presence of a fragment of the Russian requiem:

in the first movement as a reference to the tragedy.

After the death of his wife Ilya Petrovich settled down for some time with the family of his elder brother Peter, whose wife and daughters encouraged a certain amount of social entertainment, in which Peter and his school friends had their share; from all evidence it appears, in fact, that the future composer took rather more interest in the organization of merry evening parties, the invention of new games, and, above all, in dancing, than in his studies. In law he made but little progress. He hated the subject with all the bitterness that he was capable of, and he disliked only a little less the study of mathematics, for which his aptitude may be gauged by the fact that when in the fifth class he boasted that at last he had been able to solve a problem without any outside assistance, and the occurrence does not seem to have been often repeated.

In 1858 Ilya Petrovich was again a victim of over-confidence in his friends. He lost the whole of his fortune and was compelled once more to seek employment. Fortunately the influential friends he had been able to make in the capital were instrumental in securing him a most valuable post—that of director of the technical institute. On 25th May 1859 Peter Ilyich graduated from the School of Jurisprudence and was entered as an official of the first division in the Ministry of Justice. His activity there seems to have been chiefly of a negative nature. He carefully abstained from doing anything wrong, but he scarcely knew what his duties really were, and he certainly does not seem to have troubled much about them. His appreciation of serious things may be judged by an anecdote which his brother tells of him. In absent-minded moments he was apt to chew scraps of paper, and on one occasion, when he was sent from one part of the Ministry to another with a highly important document bearing the minister's own signature, he stopped to have a conversation with a friend, in the course of which he absorbed the best part of the State document. Fortunately he was able to make another copy of it, but history does not relate on what pretext he obtained a second signature. In later years he was inclined to complain that he was badly treated during his career as a State official, but there is little to show that he ever took himself seriously in that capacity. He certainly enjoyed himself at this time, although his income of fifty roubles per month can scarcely have led him into any reprehensible excesses.

His musical studies during this period are scarcely more interesting to relate than his general progress. He had many masters one after another, not one of whom had the remotest suspicion that he was assisting in the training of a young genius. One of them, Rudolf Kindinger, who was music teacher to the family, relates that he certainly had some talent, but gave little promise of rising above mediocrity, except, perhaps, in his power of improvisation, which was unusually developed and revealed a fine sense of harmony.

This facility for improvisation caused his services to be frequently in request for dance music, in which his success brought him the admiration of all the younger members of the family circle, but incidentally caused the older relations, though not his father, to treat his passion for music as something quite frivolous and contemptible. Ilya Petrovich thoroughly believed in the future of his son, and encouraged him to persevere in his musical studies.

In those days the opportunities of hearing classical music in St. Petersburg were rare, and when a symphony concert took place it was frequently given by an orchestra of amateurs playing without rehearsal, so that, in order to become acquainted with the German masterpieces, the student had to purchase them. That was before the time of cheap editions, and works which are now within the reach of the most modest purse, necessitated then an important outlay, which placed them beyond the young composer's reach. Neither could he fall back on the libraries of his friends, for the kind of music these contained was not that to which he wished to devote earnest study. It is therefore not surprising that young Tchaikovsky's musical knowledge at this date was not much more than that of a semi-cultured amateur. For instance, he appears to have had no knowledge of Schumann, and it has been stated that in 1861 he did not know how many symphonies Beethoven had composed. On the other hand, he was assiduous in his

8

visits to the Italian Opera. Russian opera was then in its infancy, and he only attended it when Glinka's *A Life for the Tsar* was performed, this having long been a favourite with him. In spite of being thus handicapped he appears to have had absolute confidence in his own future, and his brother Nicholas, who had been one of the opponents of his desire to join the musical profession, remembers that in 1862, soon after he had entered the Conservatoire, Peter said to him: 'I may not become another Glinka, but I promise you that you will some day be proud to have me for your brother.' Tchaikovsky's master at the Conservatoire was Zaremba, who was the head of the composition class, the only one which attracted the young musician. Zaremba had already privately taugh him harmony, however, before 1862. The season 1861 to 1862 was devoted to harmony after the Marx method; that of 1862 to 1863 to strict counterpoint and the church modes. From September 1863 he was studying musical form with Zaremba and orchestration with Anton Rubinstein.

In October 1862, after a journey to London, Paris, Belgium and Germany as companion and interpreter to a friend of his father's, he made the acquaintance of his fellow-student, Hermann Laroche, who became famous later on as a critic and was a firm friend of Tchaikovsky's throughout his entire career. He has much to say of the great admiration which Tchaikovsky had for Rubinstein, but this did not prevent the former from finding the restraint of the Conservatoire methods irksome. Zaremba was a classicist, and Rubinstein himself only taught the orchestration of the Mendelssohn period—that is to say, that bequeathed by Beethoven with trombones and the substitution of chromatic trumpets and horns for the natural instruments. As in all ages, the young students were carried away by their eagerness to absorb every orchestral novelty, and they were inclined to be rebellious and kick over the traces. Rubinstein's attitude of conservatism was, however, confined to his teaching, where he considered it beneficial. At the concerts of the Imperial Music Society, which he directed at that time, he conducted the works of Berlioz, Liszt and Wagner in a manner which left little doubt of his sympathy with progress. These concerts, as well as three which Wagner himself conducted when he visited St. Petersburg in 1863, naturally intensified the enthusiasm of the Conservatoire classes. It is curious that in spite of the strict rules laid down by his masters, and in spite also of his great love and admiration for Mozart, Tchaikovsky never produced a single composition for the old classical orchestra. His medium was always the expanded instrumentation of modern days.

It was customary for the students of the composition class to take away with them for the summer holidays some set task in which to test the knowledge they had acquired, and in 1864 Peter Ilyich set to work on an Overture, for which he took as programme a drama by A. N. Ostrovsky, entitled *The Storm*. Probably on the assumption that the poetic basis justified it, he went far beyond the laws of the Conservatoire, and scored merrily to his heart's content for tuba, *cor anglais,* harps, divided strings and so on. Fortunately he was unable to present the score to Rubinstein in person, for it is doubtful whether his sensitive nature could have withstood the storm which broke over the head of poor Laroche, who acted as messenger. This overture was not published until after Tchaikovsky's death, when it appeared as Op. 76.

I cannot do better than continue to quote freely from Laroche in describing the progress of Tchaikovsky's studies. No one else can have had such good opportunities of judging this, inasmuch as the two friends were in the habit of enlarging

ILYA PETROVICH TCHAIKOVSKY IN 1860
The composer's father

their acquaintance with the classics by means of copious four-hand arrangements loaned them by a friend in the publishing business, and Laroche remembers very distinctly their first impressions of new works, and particularly Tchaikovsky's at this time ever-changing likes and dislikes. In the first year they played Beethoven's ninth Symphony, the third of Schumann's, the latter's *Paradise and the Peri* and Wagner's *Lohengrin*. The young composer's preferences at this time will be disconcerting to read. They included the third Schumann Symphony, the *Ocean* Symphony of Rubinstein and two overtures by Henry Litolff, entitled *Robespierre* and *The Girondists*. At the same time he had a pronounced antipathy to Wagner, whom he on one occasion did not hesitate to place far below his own countryman Serov. Coupled with these somewhat wayward tastes were his unreasoning dislikes of certain musical combinations. For instance, he saw no beauty in that of the piano with orchestra, nor even with chamber music with stringed instruments, and was hardly less antagonistic to string quartets. He affected to have a healthy contempt for small piano pieces and songs, but it did not prevent him from admiring Schubert.

It would be wearisome to enumerate the various branches of composition to which Tchaikovsky at different times vowed that he would not contribute an iota. Only in one case did he keep his word—he did not write a violin and piano sonata.

His admiration for Serov was aroused by the latter's opera *Judith*, which held a high place in his affection until his death; but he did not entertain the same regard for this composer's later works, which, it must be admitted, were extravagant. Neither could he, of course, sympathize with Serov's ardent worship of Wagner and bitter attacks on Rubinstein and his adherents. He once visited Serov in the autumn of 1864, but does not appear to have formed a favourable opinion of his personality.

The next work to follow the unlucky *Storm* Overture consisted of some *Peasant Girls' Dances,* the performance of which at Pavlovsk that August under the direction of Johann Strauss, the waltz-king, gave him great joy. At a later date they were incorporated in his opera *The Voyevoda.* After this he wrote a string Quartet in B flat major, of which only the first movement has survived, the others having been destroyed, probably by himself. Further, an Overture in F for small orchestra, which was afterwards remodelled on a larger scale, and, according to some, lost most of its beauty in the process. The summer holiday was spent with his sister, Alexandra Davidov, at Kamenka.

In November 1865 Tchaikovsky engaged in the composition of his examination cantata on Schiller's *Ode to Joy.* The form prescribed for the occasion comprised six movements, which were as follows: (1) Orchestral introduction; (2) *Allegro,* for chorus and orchestra; (3) *Adagio,* for solo voices; (4) *Allegro,* for solos, chorus and orchestra; (5) *Andante,* for solos, chorus and orchestra; and (6) Finale, for solos, chorus and orchestra. The work was academically a success, inasmuch as it proved its author's competence, and he was declared to have satisfied the examiners, but it made no favourable impression on the musicians of the day. Rubinstein himself frankly disliked it; Serov said he had expected better; the young Russian group, through their spokesman, Cui, pronounced it weak, and only the faithful Laroche brought words of encouragement. He and Tchaikovsky seem to have mutually discovered each other. Already some years previously Tchaikovsky, impressed by his friend's conversational eloquence, had urged him to devote his attention to musical criticism, in which, as I have already mentioned, he was destined to reach the foremost rank. After the performance of the cantata we find Laroche retaliating by informing his friend in a letter that he considered him the greatest musical talent in young Russia. 'In you,' he continues, 'I see the greatest, or rather the only, hope of our musical future. Your real works will perhaps only begin five years hence, but those mature works will surpass all that we have had since Glinka.' In the same letter he proves his impartiality by severe criticism of some earlier manuscripts which Tchaikovsky had shown him, so that allowing for a certain amount of hero-worship, probably on both sides, these two men appear to have prophesied with singular accuracy each other's future.

CHAPTER II

JUST as Anton Rubinstein had founded the St. Petersburg Conservatoire, his brother Nicholas had in 1864 settled in Moscow and brought a similar institution into being there, for which at this date he required a teacher of theory. In the first place he approached Serov, but the latter was in a state of feverish elation over his brilliant but, alas! ephemeral successes, and declined the post. Thereupon Nicholas Rubinstein applied to his brother to recommend him a student capable of fulfilling the requirements, and Tchaikovsky was selected. Owing to the youth of the new Conservatoire, the position was not materially lucrative. A salary of fifty roubles a month represented presumably the same income as the young composer had contrived to live on in St. Petersburg; but as he had resigned his post at the Ministry of Justice in the spring of 1863 and had been reduced to eking out a small income by giving lessons, he must have been glad even of so small an offer. In any case the desire to have an official standing in the musical world prevailed. He signified his acceptance and left for Moscow on 17th January 1866.

Before proceeding with Tchaikovsky's Moscow experiences, it is essential to give some account of the group of interesting personalities with which he was associated there for so many years. The first place belongs naturally to the founder and head of the Conservatoire, Nicholas Rubinstein. Unlike his

14

more famous elder brother, he did not originally select a musical career, but attended Moscow University as a student of common law. His musical facilities were, however, so great that he was able at the same time to earn his living by giving piano lessons. From the time he left the university until the foundation of the Conservatoire his entire time was taken up by this teaching connection, which had assumed considerable proportions. With that important event in the musical history of Russia came his opportunity, and he revealed himself, not only as a solo pianist of high attainments, but also as a talented conductor and—what under the peculiar circumstances was perhaps the most important of all—a brilliant organizer. His ideals became identified with the existence and progress of the institution. His broad sympathies and generous temperament led him frequently to give, not only moral encouragement, but often even material assistance to the struggling young artists who were his daily care. Apart from his musicianship, he appears from all accounts to have been an extremely popular social character, with an amiable weakness for a game of cards. This probably assisted him in making the acquaintance of all the notabilities of Moscow, whom he met regularly at the English Club.

Tchaikovsky came to him as a subordinate, and this circumstance, coupled with the glamour of the name of Rubinstein and the difference of five years in their ages, caused Tchaikovsky, who was ever ready to submit to the influence of those he admired and respected, to adopt at first a somewhat deferential attitude to his chief, who at the same time was occasionally disposed to be a little imperative in his manner, although his intentions were never anything but friendly. As years went on, Tchaikovsky remained outwardly the same, mainly because it was impossible for his shy nature to allow him to assert himself, but he preserved his independence by the mental reservations he made. As a matter of fact, that was more or less his attitude towards all, and when maturity brought him self-confidence it naturally became irksome. It was this hatred of any kind of friction which led him in after years to avoid the society of his fellow men, to an extent which has caused an exaggerated view to be taken of the morbid side of his character.

Associated with Nicholas Rubinstein was Constantine Carlovich Albrecht. Laroche describes him as a mass of contradictions. His opinions always ran to extremes, and were held with a tenacity which made them unshakable. Politically he was ultra-conservative, disapproving even of the emancipation of the serfs. Musically he was, for those days, a revolutionary, all his admiration being reserved for Wagner, Liszt, Schumann and the later Beethoven. He is best remembered by his handbook on choral singing. His leisure hours were devoted to heterogeneous subjects, such as entomology, geology and mechanical invention. In the summer he was indefatigable in his hunts for butterflies and beetles, whilst the winter generally found him engaged on some intricate contrivance devoid of the slightest practical utility. He composed little, and that of no importance, but Tchaikovsky had the highest opinion of his talent, and always regretted that he had not put it to a better use. Probably he had the best opportunity of judging, as on his arrival in Moscow he boarded at first with Albrecht.

The personality of Peter Ivanovich Jurgenson deserves closer attention. He was born in 1836 at Reval, and passed his youth amidst the surroundings of poverty. At the age of nineteen he was salesman in a music shop in St. Petersburg. Having gained business experience, he went to Moscow as manager to the firm of Schildbach; but after two years the business was dissolved, and, finding himself without employment or a favourable prospect of obtaining any, he took the courageous step of founding, in 1861, a small publishing business of his own. He found a firm friend in Nicholas Rubinstein, who stood by him for twenty years. It was on his advice that the first publication, a gavotte by Bach, was selected. The following year saw the appearance of a complete edition of Mendelssohn's pianoforte works, and two years later he published a collection of Schubert's songs with Russian translations for which Rubinstein was responsible. He was thus the first to issue standard Russian editions of the great German classics, and later he was also the first to encourage the young Russian composers. Although as a business man he was not oblivious of the necessity for money-making, he did not stoop to the publication of profitable trash, and whilst his catalogue contained a large proportion of popular music, it was always of a standard which was no discredit to the publisher. The firm, which became the greatest in Russia, owned the copyrights of nearly all Tchaikovsky's works, and the relations between its founder and the composer were not at any time formal, but established on the basis of firm and even disinterested friendship.

These three men, with Kashkin, at that time professor of the piano but later a distinguished critic and one of Tchaikovsky's biographers, constituted the congenial society which the young composer found on taking up his post. Soon after his arrival they were joined by Laroche and another former fellow-student, N. A. Hubert. Until his death Tchaikovsky was always in touch with these friends, and it is largely due to their encouragement that he was enabled to lay the foundations of his fame, which they were also the first to propagate.

On his arrival in Moscow, Tchaikovsky was received by Nicholas Rubinstein with such solicitude that in one of his letters of this period he describes the latter as acting almost as a nurse. Rubinstein interested himself in all his young subordinate's little troubles, busied himself, for instance, in replenishing his wardrobe, gave him a bedroom in his house, in short, assisted him in every possible way. Under the circumstances it is not surprising that Peter Ilyich, who was at first disposed to regret his beloved St. Petersburg, gradually accommodated himself to the life of Moscow, which in later years he was wont to describe as the finest city in the world. Under Rubinstein's friendly guidance he rapidly made the acquaintance of the latter's numerous friends, who almost from the first week received him with unlimited hospitality. The letters he wrote at this time to his relations, and particularly to his favourite brothers, the twins, are full of accounts of evenings spent here and there in the most pleasant social intercourse. Nevertheless he was busy with several compositions. First of all there was the orchestration of an Overture in C minor, composed in the previous summer, to occupy him. This work did not find favour with either of the Rubinsteins, and was refused by both, as well as by another conductor to whom it was offered. Laroche was loyally enthusiastic, but the composer himself appears in course of time to have taken the view of its opponents, as at some subsequent date he inscribed the cover of the manuscript with the terse legend 'dreadful muck.' Then there was the Overture in F which has already been referred to, and which was originally written for small orchestra. At Rubinstein's request he amplified the score, but probably because of the modest nature of the original conception it was not improved by the process, and its performance at St. Petersburg was a decided failure. This larger score was eventually destroyed by him, but the original version still exists in manuscript.

Nothing daunted, he set to work on his first Symphony, in G minor (Op. 13), which bears the title *Winter Dreams*. Of all his works this one seems to have occasioned him the most trouble. He had already had to complain of a nervous affection which revealed itself mostly in the form of a hammering sensation in the head, especially in the evening, which prevented him from enjoying a healthful rest. This may have been the reason why the Symphony did not progress as he would have wished, but he himself reverses cause and effect and blames the Symphony for making him ill, for undoubtedly he did fall ill during its composition. By April 1866 he had worked himself into a most alarming condition, which resulted for a time in hallucinations, and it is significant of what he must have suffered that after this one experience he never again worked at night time. He was obliged to take a holiday, and accepted an invitation to Miatlev from his sister's mother-in-law, Mme Davidov, and her daughters Elizabeth and Vera.

In the course of the summer he paid a short visit to St. Petersburg, and, although the Symphony was not completed, he submitted it to Anton Rubinstein and Zaremba in the hope of securing its performance; but once more his work met with severe disapproval, and what was even more discouraging, the features selected for condemnation were mainly those on which he had prided himself. Returning to Moscow, he set to work to remodel the Symphony entirely. The unsympathetic manner in which his early efforts had repeatedly been received at St. Petersburg tended to lessen his affection for that town, and this feeling, coupled with an increase of his salary which was sufficient to relieve him of discomfort, soon caused him to transfer his fondness to the town in which he now felt thoroughly at home. The next musical work which engaged him was written to order. It took the form of an Overture based on the Danish National Hymn, which figures as Op. 15 in the list of his works and was composed at the request of Rubinstein to celebrate the marriage of the Tsarevich with Princess Dagmar of Denmark, the sister of Queen Alexandra. Of all his early works, this is the only one which he himself judged favourably in his maturer years. He was then disposed to be hypercritical as regards his own works of this period, but in regard to this Overture he wrote only a year before his death that he considered it not only effective, but musically superior to the well-known *1812*.

The end of 1866 found the Symphony revised and completed. He was, however, so anxious to send it to St. Petersburg in order, as he hoped, to obtain a reversal of the former unfavourable opinions, that only one movement was performed in Moscow. Unfortunately its repetition in St. Petersburg was another disappointment. Only two movements were played, and these were received with scant applause. In the press there was only one favourable voice, and that obviously an amateur's. His request for a performance of the entire work by the Imperial Russian Music Society was flatly refused by Anton Rubinstein himself. This was the last straw. Up to this point Tchaikovsky's youthful admiration for the great virtuoso had caused him to be patient and long-suffering, but everything must have its end, and with Tchaikovsky the end was always irrevocable. From that moment he never forgave Anton Rubinstein, whom he grew to consider as much an enemy as he did his brother a friend. He included in this dislike the directors of the Music Society, the press which had been unsympathetic to him and even the St. Petersburg public. It was also the last time he asked to have a work performed there.

THE COMPOSER'S BIRTHPLACE AT VOTKINSK

CHAPTER III

GROWING REPUTATION

EARLY in 1867 Tchaikovsky engaged upon the composition of his first opera, *The Voyevoda*. Progress was at first fitful and generally slow. Moreover, the composer somehow contrived to lose the libretto, which Ostrovsky had to reconstitute from memory before the work could proceed. The beginning of summer found not even an act completed. But later in the year he set to work with greater energy and soon retrieved the lost time. He incorporated in the opera, as a ballet, the *Peasant Dances* of 1865 which, long before its production in January 1869, had already achieved success in the concert-room as the *Voyevoda* Dances.

In the summer of 1867, instead of spending his holidays with his relations, he suddenly decided to take his brother Modest for a trip to Finland. They started from St. Petersburg at the beginning of June, Peter Ilyich possessing the huge sum of one hundred roubles, with which, in his simplicity, he thought they could not only stay for the entire summer, but also make an excursion to the Imatra Falls. The pair reached Viborg, where they stayed for some little while, without in the least restraining their expenditure; they also 'did' the falls, when they suddenly discovered that the balance in hand would just take them back to St. Petersburg. On their arrival in the capital they went round to their relations and found everybody out of town. Ultimately, with their last rouble, they took a steamer to Hapsal, where their sister was then staying. To this stay at Hapsal relates the title of the piano Pieces, Op. 2, which include the famous *Chant sans paroles*.

Tchaikovsky returned to Moscow in August, and the remainder of the year found him principally occupied with *The Voyevoda*, and he accommodated himself in spite of many difficulties, mainly pecuniary, to the social life of the town. The end of the year brought Berlioz on his second visit to Russia. Twenty years previously he had visited St. Petersburg, probably at the instigation of Glinka, and, incredible as it seems, the capital, saturated with inferior Italian music and scarcely knowing any other, gave him an effusive welcome. It is probable that this was due in a greater degree to his conducting and to his personality than to his works, which could scarcely appeal very vividly to the kind of audience he would have at that date. Tchaikovsky was not vastly impressed with the French composer's music, but took a great liking to him personally, regarding him as the 'personification of assiduous and disinterested energy, fiery love of art, and at the same time the most vigorous, noble combatant against ignorance, stupidity, vulgarity and routine.' Berlioz conducted two concerts at Moscow in December, one symphonic, under the auspices of the Musical Society, and one popular, given in the drill hall before an audience of twelve thousand people.

Meanwhile, in January 1867, Anton Rubinstein had resigned from the Imperial Russian Musical Society and, after some rather confused bickering, Balakirev had been appointed to the vacant conductorship. He was the central figure of the group of nationalist composers which afterwards came to be known as the 'Kutchka,' and comprised also Cui, Mussorgsky, Borodin and Rimsky-Korsakov. A letter which Tchaikovsky wrote ten years later to Mme von Meck and some references in Modist Tchaikovsky's biography give a view of his relations with the group which is somewhat distorted by events subsequent to the period under discussion. In his St. Petersburg days Tchaikovsky's musical acquaintances did not extend beyond Conservatoire circles, in which these upstarts, who made a great to-do but had not yet produced much, were generally regarded, not without some excuse, as pretentious amateurs. As we have seen, their spokesman, Cui, had dealt rather severely with Tchaikovsky's Schiller cantata, but his pen could be equally trenchant in regard to his own circle and, after all, his opinion of that work was shared by many of Tchaikovsky's friends. He had not then met any of the group. Had he done so he would have discovered that, apart from their avowed nationalism, their musical tastes were not dissimilar from his own. They shared his love of Schumann and his antipathy to Wagner. At that time they were still suspicious of Liszt, who later was to become their ally. They even concurred in Tchaikovsky's admiration for those two overtures of Litolff (see p. 11). The divergence of views which was to divide the Russian musical world into two opposed camps did not become marked until later.

One of Balakirev's first actions as conductor of the Musical Society was to send Tchaikovsky a verbal request for the score of his *Voyevoda* Dances. Tchaikovsky, still smarting, replied that before sending it he must have a written request signed by all the directors of the society. Apparently this was sent to him, for on 2nd February 1868 he writes to Balakirev: 'In accordance with our agreement I am sending you the score of my Dances; if it is possible for them to be given at some concert under your direction I shall be extremely obliged to you,' and ends his letter with a humble request for 'a little word of encouragement. Such would be in the highest degree gratifying from you.' It is evident that Tchaikovsky's somewhat unreasonable suspicions had been completely allayed. Characteristically Balakirev, who was always a procrastinating correspondent, allowed a full month to elapse before replying. Meanwhile much was happening in Moscow.

On 15th February 1868 the whole of the first Symphony was at last performed and had an extraordinary success. The composer was called for with enthusiasm and finally appeared, terribly nervous, badly dressed, holding his hat in his hand, and making the most clumsy bows. A fortnight later he made his first appearance as conductor at a charity concert, the programme of which included his *Voyevoda* Dances. Kashkin relates that in spite of all his forebodings, when he saw him in the artist's room he seemed fairly self-confident and claimed that he was not at all frightened, but when his turn came, and he timidly walked on to the platform with bowed head as if trying to hide between the desks, it was evident that his courage had not lasted. When he reached the conductor's stand he looked quite desperate. His composition had entirely escaped his memory, and he could not even see the score. He liberally distributed cues in the wrong places and to the wrong instruments. Fortunately the orchestra knew the piece well and took not the slightest notice of his baton, giving a first-rate rendering. Peter Ilyich himself declares that a feeling came over him that his head was going to drop from his shoulders and that he ought at once to put the stick down and hold it on. It was ten years before he could so far overcome his dislike of conducting as to assume responsibility again for an orchestral performance.

This same concert saw the beginning of the composer's journalistic activity. The programme had also included Rimsky-Korsakov's *Fantasy on Serbian Themes*, and one of

TCHAIKOVSKY IN 1863

the newspapers, which spoke warmly of Tchaikovsky, attacked this piece with most depressing adjectives. As his brother points out, a few months previously Tchaikovsky might perhaps have taken no notice of this, but from the recent correspondence with Balakirev he had acquired the certitude that these men were far from being unfriendly. Moreover, he had been present at the several rehearsals of the piece in question and been favourably impressed by it. He promptly launched out a vigorous denunciation of the offending critic which made quite a stir in Moscow and was much appreciated by the St. Petersburg group.

Two days after this concert Balakirev replied acknowledging receipt of the Dances, but expressing regret that it would be impossible to perform them that season, as it was too late. His letter concludes:

As for the word of encouragement . . . encouragement is only for the little children of art, whereas your score shows me that you are a mature artist worthy of *severe criticism*. When we meet I shall be very glad to give you my opinion; but it would be impossible in a letter, for the letter would grow into an entire essay, and that from my unliterary pen would be deadly. It would be far better to play through the piece together at the piano and criticize it bar by bar.

The meeting came about sooner than either expected, for at Easter Tchaikovsky found time to spend a few days at St. Petersburg. Dargomizhsky's house was then the meeting-place of the nationalist group. Balakirev took Tchaikovsky there and introduced him to Cui, Rimsky-Korsakov and Stassov, who was destined to become the historian of the movement. In his *Memoirs* Rimsky-Korsakov says: 'He showed himself to be a pleasant companion, with a sympathetic personality. His manner was simple and natural and he always appeared to speak with warmth and sincerity. On the first evening of our acquaintance Balakirev got him to play the first movement of his G minor Symphony, which pleased us very much.' He soon made friends with the group, particularly with 'Korsinka' (Rimsky-Korsakov). For the next four years at least relations were as close as they can be between busy people separated by distance.

In the summer Tchaikovsky accepted an offer to travel with his pupil, Vladimir Shilovsky, and his tutor, continuing the former's musical lessons. They spent a week in Berlin and then made Paris their headquarters. The style in which they lived was very pleasant to Tchaikovsky, who could never afford so much luxury at home, but nevertheless, a letter he wrote at this time admits that he would have preferred to be with his relations in the country, living a quiet and peaceful life of daily congenial work. During the whole of this time, up to September 1868, he did not touch any other compositions than his opera, on which he built such great hopes.

Meanwhile his material circumstances had been vastly improved by an important increase in the number of his pupils. The ensuing freedom from care encouraged him to proceed with great energy with the composition of *The Voyevoda,* of which rehearsals soon began to take place. Apart from this the composer's life was not very eventful, but some interest attaches to his acquaintance with the singer Désirée Artôt, who visited Russia as the star of an operatic company. She was the daughter of a famous horn player and the niece of a great violinist. Her training she owed partly to Mme Viardot-Garcia, and partly to Lamperti. She was a very fascinating woman, and as an artist she was much admired, not only for her singing, but for her dramatic power and versatility, which enabled her to interpret with true emotion a wide range of vocal music.

The young composer, then twenty-eight years old, became greatly infatuated with her, as the following correspondence will show. On 2nd November 1868 he wrote to his sister thus:

I am terribly busy just now, arranging the recitatives and choruses of Auber's *Black Domino,* which is to be given on A——t's benefit night; for this work I hope to get paid. I have made great friends with A——t, and am favoured with her special regard. Never in my life have I met such a sweet, such a warm-hearted, such an intellectual woman. Anton Rubinstein has been to see us again. He played like a god and created a great furore. He has not changed in the least and is as good-natured as ever. I often frequent the Musical Society now and play yeralash at half-kopek points. After our game, Givochini, Ostrovsky, Sadovsky and I sup together. They are three jolly good fellows. I have completed an orchestral fantasy, *Fatum.* . . .

And the following month to his brother Modest:

Ah, my dear brother Modest, I am overwhelmed with a need to disburden my heart to your sympathetic, comprehending soul. If only you could realize what an artist and what a singer A——t is! I have never been so deeply moved and stirred by any vocalist before! I am so grieved that you can neither see her nor hear her! How thoroughly delighted you would be with her exquisite gestures, with her grace of movement, her artistic pose!

In December his enthusiasm for her as an artist developed into love for her as a woman, and he began to contemplate matrimony. In fact, in another letter to his brother, he excuses himself for his dilatoriness in replying to the latter's letters on the ground that he devoted every spare moment he had to a 'certain person' whom he loved dearly. Very soon he considered the moment had arrived to consult his father, to whom he wrote as follows:

MY DEAR, GOOD FATHER,—To my intense grief, circumstances interfere with my coming to see you at Petersburg. The journey would cost at the very least 100 roubles; besides, I have not the time at present to undertake it. Thus separated from you, I send you my hearty New Year's greetings; needless to say, I wish you every happiness and God's blessing. Reports of my intended marriage have no doubt reached you, and you will perhaps have felt hurt that I did not at once write and inform you of it myself. I will now try to explain the whole affair to you. I became acquainted with A——t in the spring, though I had not visited her more than once at her house to supper; it was the night of her benefit concert. On her return here this autumn I never so much as saw her till we happened to meet at a musical evening. She expressed some surprise that I had not called upon her, and I promised that I would. At the time I really had no intention of doing so—you know my peculiar shyness with new acquaintances —but it happened that Anton Rubinstein was just then passing through Moscow, and he induced me to visit her. From that time forth I was in the receipt of most pressing letters from her almost daily, and by degrees—I know not how—I dropped into the way of visiting her constantly. We rapidly became enamoured of each other. The question of our marriage has naturally been touched upon, and we both wish it to take place in the summer, if nothing should hinder it. But I must confess that there are certain impediments which *do* threaten to hinder it. First, her mother, who is continually with her, and who possesses great influence over her daughter, is against the marriage; she considers me too young for A——t, and she fears that in all probability I shall insist on her daughter living in Russia. Secondly, my friends, especially Nicholas Rubinstein, are using their utmost endeavours to prevent this marriage. They maintain that in marrying so famous a singer I should have to play the humiliating part of being merely my wife's husband—i.e. that I should have to follow her about in every corner of Europe, that I should have to live at her expense, and finally I should have to dissociate myself from work, or rather have no opportunity of serious work. In a word, that when the honeymoon of my passion for my wife was subdued there would follow injured vanity, despair and ruin. It might, perhaps, be possible to forestall such a tragic denouement if she were to leave the stage and settle to live here in Russia with me; but she tells me that, with all her intense love for me, she could never consent to forsake a profession to which she is so wedded, and which is bringing her both fame and fortune. She is now in Warsaw, and so we have agreed to postpone our final decision for a while until I rejoin her at her home near Paris. She feels she cannot leave the stage— good. I likewise for my own part cannot but hesitate to sacrifice my whole future prospects for her. For there can hardly be a doubt that I should destroy my chances of a career if I were to follow her blindly. And so, dear father, you will see that I am somewhat in a fix. On the one hand, I am, I may say, attached to her, body and soul, and my life seems a blank without her; on the other hand, cold stern philosophy compels me to reflect upon the disastrous consequences which may ensue, and which my friends continue to impress upon me with earnestness. I await your own view of the matter, dearest father. I am quite well, and my days pursue their usual course, with the only difference that she is away from me at this moment, and I am sick at heart without her.

The reply ran:

You ask advice, dear Peter, upon a momentous crisis in your career. Truly, *mon ami*, marriage is such a vitally important step in life that one should not venture to take it without cool and mature reflection. It is a question of life and death, a 'to be or not to be,' a gambler's final stake, a brave man's last hazard! From such a step there is no receding, albeit youthful ardent natures are apt to venture on it rashly, guided merely by their own cravings, with never a thought of the moral and the religious responsibilities entailed therein. In the short note which I enclosed in Toli's [Anatol's] letter to you you will find my own views regarding this marriage of yours. I rejoice—I rejoice as the father of a grown-up son—I rejoice at the proposed marriage of one who is worthy to the most worthy of him. You love each other! Good; the affair lies in a nutshell. *But*—oh! that accursed word 'but'—we must reflect, we must dissect this Gordian knot thread by thread. Désirée, the 'wished-for one,' must, of course, be beautiful in all respects, since my son Peter is in love with her; for my son Peter is a man of taste, a man of intellect, a man of superior qualities, and if we judge him by his merits we shall expect him to select a wife of the same traits and character as himself. As to the fitness of age, of that there is no question. You are both of age, and two years either way are a trivial difference in this case. But as regards your mutual means and position, well, a little investigation is certainly most necessary. You are an artist, and so is she; both of you are aiming at turning your talents into a fortune. She has, however, already acquired both fortune and fame, whereas you are only struggling to attain both, and God knows whether you will ever attain what she already possesses. Your friends recognize your talent, but fear lest you should sacrifice it by this change of life. I do not, however, share their anxiety. You are proud, and chafe at not having sufficient means to maintain a wife—to be independent of her purse. Yes, *mon ami,* I quite understand your feelings. Yet surely, if you both set to work and earn money together, you will both be independent of each other. Go your way, and let your wife pursue hers, and you will mutually help each other. I do not advise either of you to forsake your profession; but I see no reason whatever why you should not marry each other and be thoroughly happy. . . . As to her mother, I do not think she need be considered or admitted to interfere in your love affairs.[1]

There is no record of the composer having replied to his

[1] The translation of this interesting correspondence is by Miss A. E. Keeton.

father, and the brief but tempestuous love affair ended abruptly within a month by the lady's marrying a popular baritone singer, Mariano Padilla, at Warsaw, without offering the composer any explanation. Shortly afterwards she revisited Moscow, and Tchaikovsky, to whom she had caused so much pain, sat in the stalls with the tears streaming down his face. It is quite possible that she was the greatest love of his life, but it was nearly a quarter of a century before they met again. That was in Berlin, and they greeted each other as old friends.

The Voyevoda was produced on 11th February 1869. Another opera, *Undine,* was completed before the end of July, after which the composer spent most of the summer at Kamenka, where the occasion of a gathering of the family proved that Peter Ilyich had not as yet lost any of his boyishness. He entered into the spirit of all the fun his younger brothers indulged in, emulated them in jumping ditches, and was the ringleader in building bonfires in the woods. Returning to Moscow in the autumn he again met Balakirev, who spent a few days there, mostly in his company and that of Borodin. The first result of this visit was the dedication to Balakirev of the Symphonic Poem *Fatum*; the second and more important result, the composition of the Fantasy-Overture *Romeo and Juliet,* which, as we shall see later, was the direct outcome of the conversations and correspondence between the two composers. This work occupied most of his time in the autumn, but at the urgent request of the publisher Bessel he consented to do a piano duet arrangement of Anton Rubinstein's Overture to *Ivan the Terrible.* At the same time he was busy with the preparation of a new course of lessons in musical form, but as these were solely for use in his classes it is doubtful whether they have been preserved in any shape or form. The following January Balakirev returned to Moscow, this time in the company of Rimsky-

Korsakov, and, as might be expected, the three were continually together. It also appears that mutual admiration was the rule, for whilst the visitors were more and more enchanted with Tchaikovsky, and especially with *Romeo,* the latter was almost equally delighted with Korsakov's songs, one of which was then dedicated to him. The high opinion of *Romeo* was shared by everybody in Moscow, and Nicholas Rubinstein succeeded in obtaining its immediate publication by the important firm of Bote & Bock in Berlin. In November he submitted the opera *Undine,* which was refused by the authorities, who added insult to injury by mislaying the score. It was, however, subsequently discovered, but only to be destroyed by the composer himself, who by that time had come to the conclusion that for once the authorities were right. Certain fragments, however, as we shall see later, survived in other forms.

CHAPTER IV

FULL MATURITY

Before proceeding with our story it will be expedient to dispose of the question of Tchaikovsky's attitude to the 'Kutchka.' A large portion of the history of modern Russian music is occupied with the rivalries of the two opposed schools of musical thought, that of the self-styled nationalists of St. Petersburg and that of the Moscow circle whose members were subsequently described abroad, but rarely in Russia, as eclectics. Though Tchaikovsky made occasional use of folksong, he never espoused the nationalist creed. He had a great esteem for Balakirev, whom he regarded as the outstanding personality of the group. He also thought highly of Rimsky-Korsakov. He saw talent in Borodin and deplored that it should be wasted. He thought Mussorgsky flirted with coarseness as Cui flirted with elegance. On their side the members of the group were not slow in appreciating his genius, and they attempted as opportunity presented itself to convert him to their musical religion. Three of his symphonic poems: *Fatum, Romeo and Juliet* and *The Tempest,* the first two dedicated to Balakirev, the last-named to Stassov, show traces of these attempts to bring him into the fold. Tchaikovsky was also sufficiently large-minded to advocate in later years the performance in Moscow of the works of the group even when he disapproved of them. This was not, however, always the case, as he thoroughly believed in the talent at least of Balakirev and Rimsky-Korsakov, and only considered that the group had contrived to lose its way in its search for truth. In 1872 Balakirev seceded from the group, which from that time began gradually to lose its solidarity whilst remaining for some time longer faithful to its tenets. Ten years later Balakirev gave Tchaikovsky the incentive to the composition of his *Manfred* Symphony. Their friendship endured, but afterwards Balakirev became more and more a recluse, taking greater interest in religious matters than in music, though towards the end of his long life he emerged from his self-imposed solitude and engaged upon the revision of his early works. By then, however, Tchaikovsky's career was ended.

In the later pages of this volume, which will be devoted to a consideration of Tchaikovsky's works, the circumstances under which each composition was produced will be referred to at some length. It is therefore necessary to confine ourselves for the present to purely biographical matter. As to that, we are entering upon a period of the composer's life which was somewhat uneventful. There was the daily round of lessons at the Conservatoire, the yearly outburst of creative energy during the recess, an occasional first performance, but little else. The success of the Conservatoire naturally influenced the young composer's income, which, whilst still modest, assumed dimensions which rendered life fairly free from anxiety. It is in singular contrast with the pessimism which is generally ascribed to Tchaikovsky that he regarded each successive increase of his emoluments as representing wealth. His brother relates that about this time he calculated that he was earning 1,441 roubles, and he promptly came to the conclusion that he could afford to leave Nicholas Rubinstein's roof and set up his own establishment. Fortunately for him his host persuaded him to remain for the time being.

From now on until 1877 the only event worth chronicling is that Tchaikovsky, after two abortive attempts to separate himself from Nicholas Rubinstein, succeeded in doing so. It is recorded that there was some little friction between the two, and it is beyond a doubt that as his genius developed, the domineering personality of the elder musician must have exercised an irksome, even if unconscious, tyranny on Peter Ilyich, who was too sensitive and shy to take his own part in their conversations. The episode of the piano Concerto, to be referred to later, was only one of several which made the separation desirable.

Otherwise the composer's movements during this period may be briefly summarized as follows. In January 1870 he wrote a chorus for an opera, *Mandragora,* which, however, he abandoned. The following month he began a new work for the stage, *The Oprichnik.* After learning the fate of his opera *Undine* he was suddenly called to Paris, where his friend and former pupil Shilovsky was lying dangerously ill. After three days they left together for Soden, a little village at the foot of the Taunus, where they arrived at the end of May. Tchaikovsky attended the Beethoven Centenary Festival at Mannheim and visited Nicholas Rubinstein at Wiesbaden, where the latter had just gambled away his last rouble. The outbreak of the Franco-Prussian War drove the friends to Interlaken, where Tchaikovsky spent six weeks. Towards the end of August he returned via Munich and Vienna to St. Petersburg and thence to Moscow in time for the autumn term at the Conservatoire. The following March, 1871, at the first performance of his D major Quartet, he became acquainted with Turgenev. In the summer of 1873 he spent another holiday abroad, visiting Breslau, Dresden, Cologne, Zürich, Lucerne, Berne, Vevey, Geneva, Milan, Cadenabbia and

Paris. The following spring took him again to Italy. In March 1875 Shilovsky attended the first performance of Bizet's *Carmen* in Paris and was so impressed that he forwarded a piano score to Tchaikovsky, who became equally enthusiastic. In November Saint-Saëns came to Moscow. Though their friendship was not to endure, the two composers became for the time being so intimate that they indulged in an amusing frolic. Being both enamoured of ballet they performed one in private on the stage of the Conservatoire. It was called *Galathea and Pygmalion*. Nicholas Rubinstein officiated 'at the piano,' Saint-Saëns represented the statue which Tchaikovsky as Pygmalion brought to life. At the end of December Peter Ilyich accompanied his brother Modest to Paris, where they saw *Carmen* together. Tchaikovsky returned almost immediately to Russia, but in July 1876 he was ordered to Vichy, whence, after 'taking the waters,' he proceeded to Bayreuth. Here he became acquainted with Liszt and called on Wagner, who had, however, ceased to receive visitors. In a letter to his brother he declares that after hearing the last chords of *Götterdämmerung* he felt as if he had been released from a prison, and adds 'how many thousand times finer is the ballet of *Sylvia*!' He was willing to admit that the *Ring* contained a large number of episodes of a symphonic character handled in a masterly manner, but to his mind this could not compensate for long periods of absolute dullness. One of his aversions, in particular, was Wotan's long, reproachful address to Brünnhilde on her disobedience. Apart from these few journeys the whole story of these eight years is to be sought in the chronological list of his works.

The year 1877 is a cardinal point in Tchaikovsky's life, inasmuch as it brought with it the two events which had the greatest influence upon his subsequent career. To begin with the one destined to yield the most beneficial results, we must refer to the extraordinary friendship which grew up between the young composer and a lady who was an ardent admirer of his works, Mme Nadezhda Filaretovna von Meck, the widow of a well-known railway engineer who had recently died and left her a considerable fortune. She was then nearing her forty-sixth birthday. He first came into communication with her through the medium of a young violinist who attended his composition classes and was occasionally engaged to play at her house. The student was never weary of singing his master's praises, and in Mme von Meck he found a delighted listener. After a time she commissioned the composer to make one or two arrangements of his own works for her use, and the necessary discussion of details led to a protracted correspondence, which is preserved almost in its entirety in the voluminous biography by Modest Tchaikovsky. Most of what we know of Tchaikovsky's attitude towards his own compositions can be gathered there, as well as many interesting impressions of his various musical travels.

With admirable delicacy Mme von Meck insisted from the very beginning that they should not meet. Her reason was partly that she wished to preserve intact the impression of Tchaikovsky she derived from his works, which might have been clouded by some trifle had their relations ever become personal; at least that was the reason which she wished to be believed; but, considering that she was affording him substantial material assistance, it is far more likely that she wished to spare his sensitive nature the least feeling of obligation. This material assistance at first took the form of liberal fees for the transcriptions she requested, but before many months were over, an arrangement was made whereby Tchaikovsky received a fixed income of six thousand roubles yearly, sufficient to render him free to devote himself entirely to composition. It is impossible to speak too highly of her conduct in the matter. There have been patrons of music before. Art has at all times been kept alive by wealth, but seldom in the history of art has wealth played its part in so tasteful and discreet a manner. The condition that they should not meet was kept to the letter. It was of course unavoidable that they should sometimes be simultaneously present in the same concert-hall or theatre, but even then they passed as strangers, and, as the composer's brother puts it, to the end neither heard the other's voice.

Mme von Meck frequently went to France, where she stayed at the château of Chenonceau. Whilst on a visit there in the spring of 1879 she wrote to Marmontel at the Paris Conservatoire to ask if he could recommend her one of his pupils as 'house pianist,' to take part in piano duets and in trios for piano, violin and cello. In response Marmontel sent her a talented youth in his seventeenth year who travelled in her company to Florence, Venice and Vienna, and finally to Moscow. One of his first tasks was to arrange for piano three dances from Tchaikovsky's ballet, *The Swan Lake*. The name of this talented young pianist was Claude Debussy.

The other event of 1877 was the composer's unfortunate marriage. In the spring of that year, whilst engaged upon the fourth Symphony, which, when completed, was to be dedicated to Mme von Meck, he began to look for a likely subject for his next opera. As we shall see when dealing with it, Elizabeth Andreievna Lavrovskaya, singer and professor at the Moscow Conservatoire, drew his attention to that of Pushkin's *Eugene Oniegin*. The suggestion took root, and without waiting for the libretto which Shilovsky undertook to write for him, he set to work upon Tatiana's 'letter scene,' which had an extraordinary fascination for him. About the same time he had received a long letter, containing a passionate declaration of love, signed Antonina Ivanovna Milyukov. She said that her love had originated some years before when she was a pupil at the Conservatoire, but he had no recollection of her. Busy as he was, he put the letter aside and dismissed it from his mind. Presently a second letter arrived. Meanwhile he had become completely immersed in his opera. Tatiana had his entire sympathy and he thought Oniegin a cold, heartless coxcomb. Miss Milyukov's second letter overwhelmed him with the same reproaches which he, in imagination, was addressing to Oniegin, and threatened suicide if he did not reply. The analogy of the situation affected him so deeply that he called upon her. He informed her that he had only friendship to offer her in return for her love, but his visit, in itself an imprudence, merely added fuel to the flame. In his mind there was constantly that feeling of indignation at Oniegin's careless, thoughtless attitude to Tatiana. Fatalist as he was, he thought he felt the hand of destiny, and eventually he declared himself willing to marry her. Even then he made no protestations of love, painted himself in the darkest colours, dwelt at length on his nervous and uncertain temperament and his poor prospects. He bound her to secrecy, left all the arrangements to her and, regarding the matter as settled, spent nearly the whole of June at Glebovo with Shilovsky, working at the opera. Presently a letter came from Antonina reminding him of his engagement. He broke the news to his family, whose reception of it left nothing to be desired, and Ilya Petrovich, who was then eighty-three years old, hastened by letter to welcome the prospective bride as a daughter. The marriage took place on 18th July 1877.

As far as worldly wisdom can judge, a marriage entered

upon under such circumstances was bound to end in failure. From the very first day it was evident that grave circumstances had caused him to regret the step he had taken, and on 7th August he wrote that a few more days of such life would have driven him mad. He then spent some little time away from his wife at Kamenka, but returned early in September to Moscow, where she had prepared a home for him. Life together proved altogether intolerable, and before the end of the month he left suddenly for St. Petersburg on the pretext of a telegram. He arrived there in a state of absolute collapse, and had to be taken at once to the hotel nearest the station, where he had a nervous attack which ended in his being unconscious for forty-eight hours. Then followed a week of high fever, after which, the doctors having decided that a complete change was necessary to restore his health, he left Russia, reaching Berlin on 15th October. From there he proceeded to Clarens, a quiet little spot on Lake Geneva, well calculated to effect a cure in such a case as his.

The circumstances which brought about this crisis in the composer's life are such that one does not like to discuss them at any length. Rumours of various kinds have been circulated in and out of Russia, reflecting on the character and morality now of the husband, now of the wife, but nothing has transpired which affords them the slightest foundation. Tchaikovsky, if his own later writings are to be believed, was most anxious to exonerate his wife from all blame and to ascribe the tragedy to the perversity of fate, which had thrown together two utterly incompatible natures. When he complains, it is not of his wife, but of his inability to work in her presence, the reason for which may have been as much in himself as in her. His exaggerated sensitiveness is well known, and it is quite possible that occurrences which to a man of different fibre would have been at the worst irritating pin-pricks, were unendurable tortures to him. However, under the unfortunate circumstances, the only possible solution was the separation which accordingly took place, but in view of much that has been hinted in connection with the marriage, it is advisable, at the risk of tedious repetition, to remind the reader that, beyond complaining of mutual incompatibility, Tchaikovsky never to the day of his death permitted himself to speak with harshness of the lady who was his wife, and she, on her side, declares in her reminiscences that 'Peter was in no way to blame.'

At Clarens he hired a villa, and finding that the money he had in hand was barely sufficient for five or six weeks, he wrote to his friends in Moscow. It was in response to this that the generous offer of Mme von Meck above referred to was made, and almost at the same time a letter from Nicholas Rubinstein set Tchaikovsky's mind at rest regarding his position at the Conservatoire, from which payments were to be made to him at least for a year of his stay abroad.

From Clarens he journeyed to Italy, where he first stayed at San Remo and afterwards in Florence; but to judge by his letters, it would seem that the joy was marred by coming at the wrong moment. To Kashkin he writes: 'Our going to Italy was pure folly. Her riches, her dazzling beauty, only made me irritable and worried me. I had no heart left to appreciate her great monuments, which left me cold and indifferent.'[1]

The rest of the time was occupied with flying visits to Paris, Vienna and other places, where he attended many concerts, and heard works which at that date were unknown in Russia. He was much attracted in France by the music of Bizet and Delibes, but his musical recollections of his visit to Vienna

[1] Rosa Newmarch's translation.

41

were not so pleasant, being associated with Wagner's *Ring*, and the music of Brahms, for neither of which he had any appreciation.

It is much easier to understand the Russian composer's aversion to Brahms than to Wagner, for it would be impossible to conceive two composers of more opposite temperaments. All the racial antagonism of the Teuton and the Slav is expressed in this antipathy, which is known to have been mutual. On the one side, music calm, intellectual, *raisonnée*, of careful and calculated symmetry; on the other, passion, the coursing of warm blood, the violent reactions of an emotional temperament, fringing hysteria both in its exuberance and in its depression. Mutual admiration in such a case could only have engendered suspicion as to its genuineness.

Towards the end of 1877 Tchaikovsky was approached with an offer of the appointment to take charge of the section of Russian music at the Paris exhibition of 1878. Most reluctantly he accepted it, but almost immediately afterwards changed his mind. The reason for this was that he found that his duties would necessarily bring him into personal contact with a large number of people he did not know. The mere thought of such a thing appalled him. In resigning the post, he was careful to explain that it was not unwillingness or laziness which caused him to do so, but this uncomfortable shyness, which he describes as an unconquerable disease. The following spring, after a return to Clarens, he returned to Russia, and having spent some time in the country, resumed his classes at the Conservatoire for a short while. He had announced his intention of continuing them as usual, but the attraction of his newly found liberty was too much for him, and he soon gave them up in order to devote himself exclusively to composition.

CHAPTER V

THE LAST YEARS

ONCE free, Tchaikovsky began absenting himself from Moscow with much greater frequency. Apart from spending the summer in the country, he rarely passed a year without a journey abroad, now to Clarens, to which he grew much attached, now to France, Germany or Italy.

In March 1881 Nicholas Rubinstein died. Tchaikovsky was offered the directorship of the Conservatoire, but felt himself unsuited to the post and declined. During the following winter he wrote the Trio 'to the memory of a great artist.'

Early in 1885, after many disappointments, Tchaikovsky at last found a country house to suit his temperament. It was situated in the village of Maidanovo, a couple of versts from the town of Klin. From then onwards he lived the hermit life which he preferred to all others, emerging from his solitude with some reluctance for those triumphal tours which the spread of his fame now imposed upon him. His establishment there was quite modest. Apart from the fact that his means, though sufficient for comfort, would not have justified any display, his own tastes were as simple as possible. The management of the household was left entirely to his servant Sofronov, the composer being as innocent as a child of such matters. His brother relates that if by any chance he ever did purchase anything for the house it was invariably of monumental uselessness.   On the same authority we know his mode of living at that time, which was regularity itself.   He rose between seven and eight and drank tea, mostly without anything to eat.   He then read for some time, generally works of a philosophical character, or some such book as Otto Jahn's biography of Mozart.   If he was engaged on any serious study, such as that of the English language, which he began to learn in the last few years of his life, it was this time that was devoted to it.   Then he would go for a short walk, and his intentions for the day were now patent to those who knew him.   If he had breakfasted in silence, and started for his walk alone, it meant that he would commence work on his return.   If he began the day in a talkative mood, and walked with a friend, it meant that there would be no work done beyond perhaps the reading of a few proofs.   He dined at one o'clock and invariably went for another walk imme‑ diately after, returning about four o'clock for tea.   From five to seven he worked again, after which the evening was generally spent in social intercourse.

It was on these walks that the real creative work of composi‑ tion was done.   He was all his life a great lover of nature, and at his happiest in the open air, so much so that he himself thought he had not found the real musical impression he sought until he was able to do all his work in that way.   The pro‑ gramme Symphony of *Manfred* marks the end of the old days, being the last work not thought out in complete solitude.

At the end of 1887 the composer left Russia for a three months' tour in Western Europe.   There exists a vivid account of this journey in the form of a diary which has been admirably translated by Rosa Newmarch and appears at the end of the book which she published in 1900.   This narrative is so interesting a document that did space allow one would be

44

tempted to include it in its entirety—in fact, a biography of Tchaikovsky on a large scale would not be complete if it did not contain every line of it; but as the purpose of this book is not solely biographical,[1] but also introductory to the works of the master, it is necessary to condense the matter considerably.

The circumstance which led Tchaikovsky to take what was for him the momentous step of facing unremitting publicity for three months was the fact that he had just made quite a successful appearance as a conductor, first at the production of one of his own operas, and immediately afterwards at a symphony concert. Rightly or wrongly he had always assumed that his intense nervousness utterly disqualified him from ever handling the conductor's baton, and certainly his tentative efforts in this direction earlier in his career had not been encouraging, but on these two occasions he discovered, greatly to his own astonishment, that it was quite possible for him to control an orchestra. He did not become a great conductor, even of his own works—indeed it was not to be expected when one considers that he was forty-seven years of age at the time in question, but it is recorded that his interpretation fell little behind the standard set by the great professional conductors.

He left St. Petersburg at the end of December for Berlin. Here a shock awaited him. Picking up a newspaper at his hotel he found to his horror that a well-meaning but over-zealous agent had arranged a luncheon in his honour, at which musical Berlin was expected to be present to welcome him. Considering that at this period musical Berlin knew practically nothing about him, and was not predisposed to be sympathetic to a Slav composer, Tchaikovsky judged that to become a party to this arrangement would lay him open to a charge of

[1] Some additional biographical matter will be found in the Calendar, Appendix A.

pretentiousness, surely the last vice of which any one could accuse him. In sheer fright he escaped to Leipzig without seeing anybody except the agent, whom he confesses he would willingly have murdered.

At Leipzig, he spent some very happy days in the company of his fellow-countrymen Brodsky, the violinist, and Siloti, the pianist, whom he knew already, and made the interesting acquaintance of Brahms, Grieg, Delius, Busoni and others. It was here that he saw Désirée Artôt again, nearly twenty years after their fateful meeting. She was now fifty-three. His description of Brahms is as follows:

Brahms is a rather short man, suggests a sort of amplitude, and possesses a very sympathetic appearance. His fine head, almost that of an old man, recalls the type of a handsome, benign, elderly Russian priest. His features are certainly characteristic of Russian good looks, and I cannot conceive why some learned ethnographer (Brahms himself told me this after I had spoken of the impression his appearance made upon me) chose to reproduce his head on the first page of one of his books as being highly characteristic of German features. A certain softness of outline, pleasing curves, rather long and slightly grizzled hair, kind grey eyes, and a thick beard, freely sprinkled with white—all this at once recalled the type of pure-bred Great Russian, so frequently met with among our clergy.

Brahms's manner is very simple, free from vanity, his humour jovial, and the few hours spent in his society left me with a very agreeable recollection.

This of his personality, but of his music he writes in a different vein:

There is something dry, cold, vague and nebulous in the music of this master which is repellent to Russian hearts. From our Russian point of view Brahms does not possess melodic invention. His musical ideas never speak to the point; hardly have we heard

46

an allusion to some tangible melodic phrase, than it disappears in a whirlpool of almost unmeaning harmonic progressions and modulations, as though the composer's special aim were to be incomprehensible and obscure. Thus he excites and irritates our musical perceptions, as it were, yet is unwilling to satisfy their demands; he seems ashamed, to put it plainly, to speak clearly and reach the heart. Hearing his music, we ask ourselves: Is Brahms deep, or does he only desire to have the semblance of depth in order to mask the poverty of his imagination? This question is never satisfactorily answered. It is impossible in listening to Brahms's music to say that it is weak or unremarkable. His style is always elevated. Unlike all our contemporary musicians, he never has recourse to purely external effects; he never attempts to astonish us, to strike us by some new and brilliant orchestral combination; nor do we meet in his music with anything trivial or directly imitative. It is all very serious, very distinguished, apparently, even original, but in spite of all this the chief thing is lacking—beauty.

It is interesting to contrast with the above what he writes of Grieg, a composer whose works attracted him from the earliest stages of his acquaintance with them:

In his music there prevails that fascinating melancholy which seems to reflect in itself all the beauty of Norwegian scenery, now grandiose and sublime in its vast expanse, now grey and dull, but always full of charm to the hearts of Northmen, and having something akin to ourselves, quickly finds its way to our hearts, and evokes a warm and sympathetic response. Grieg is probably not by any means so great a master as Brahms; his range is not so extensive, his aims and tendencies are not so wide, and apparently in Grieg the inclination towards obscurity is entirely absent; nevertheless he stands nearer to us, he seems more approachable and intelligible because of his deep humanity. Hearing the music of Grieg we instinctively recognize that it was written by a man impelled by an irresistible impulse to give vent by means of sounds to a flood of poetical emotion, which obeys no theory or principle, is stamped

47

with no impress but that of a vigorous and sincere artistic feeling. Perfection of form, strict and irreproachable logic in the development of his themes, are not perseveringly sought after by the celebrated Norwegian. But what charm, what inimitable and rich musical imagery! What warmth and passion in his melodic phrases, what teeming vitality in his harmony, what originality and beauty in the turn of his piquant and ingenious modulations and rhythms, and in all the rest what interest, novelty and independence! If we add to all this that rarest of qualities, a perfect simplicity, far removed from affectation and pretence to obscurity and far-fetched novelty, it is not surprising that every one should delight in Grieg.

One more quotation concerning the composer's new acquaintances at Leipzig forces itself upon us here, because the subject of it happens to be a countrywoman of our own, who afterwards justified the opinion that Tchaikovsky formed of her by becoming one of the most eminent of British composers.

After the Christmas Tree, while we were all sitting round the tea-table, at Brodsky's, a beautiful dog of the setter breed came bounding into the room and began to frisk round the host and his little nephew, who welcomed his arrival. 'This means that Miss Smyth will appear directly,' everybody exclaimed at once, and in a few minutes a tall Englishwoman, not handsome, but having what people call an 'expressive' or 'intelligent' face, walked into the room, and I was introduced to her at once as a fellow composer. Miss Smyth is one of the comparatively few women composers who may be seriously reckoned among the workers in this sphere of music. She had come to Leipzig a few years before, and studied theory and composition very thoroughly; she had composed several interesting works (the best of which, a violin sonata, I heard excellently played by the composer herself and Mr. Brodsky), and gave promise in the future of a serious and talented career. Since no Englishwoman is without her originalities and eccentricities, Miss Smyth had hers, which were: the beautiful dog, which was quite inseparable from this lonely woman, and invariably announced her arrival, not only on this occasion, but at other times when I met her again; a passion for hunting, on account of which Miss Smyth occasionally returned to England for a time; and, finally, an incomprehensible and almost passionate worship for the intangible musical genius of Brahms. From her point of view, Brahms stood on the supreme pinnacle of all music, and all that had gone before him served merely as a preparation for the incarnation of absolute musical beauty in the creations of the Viennese master.

During Tchaikovsky's stay at Leipzig, his first Suite was performed at the Gewandhaus, and the Liszt-Verein gave a concert consisting solely of his works, the *pièce de résistance* being the Trio, which was splendidly rendered by Siloti, Haliř and Schroeder. The composer's visits to Hamburg, Berlin and Prague were equally successful, but there is little to record of them, except that in Prague he made the acquaintance of Dvořák. In Paris, to all outward appearances, he was even more warmly welcomed, and was considered quite the man of the moment. In a novel, the publication of which coincided with his visit, his song 'Nur wer die Sehnsucht kennt' was used as a kind of *leitmotiv* to the plot. Unfortunately the Paris musical public is fickle, and Tchaikovsky never succeeded in gaining as firm a hold on it as some of his compatriots, such as Rimsky-Korsakov and Borodin. The intense nationalism of these composers appealed to the French public more vividly than Tchaikovsky's eclecticism, and his reputation there never reached the height to which it attained in other countries, notably our own.

However, his brother Modest writes rather frigidly of his stay in London, which lasted only four days. The credit for this visit is due to the Philharmonic Society and its then secretary, Francesco Berger. The latter's invitation to his house appears to be the only one the composer accepted—indeed, his brother almost leads one to believe that it was the only one he received. The works performed were his Serenade for strings and the Variations from the third Suite, both of which were well received, although there was little to foreshadow the enormous popularity the composer was to enjoy later in this country.

From the moment that Tchaikovsky accustomed himself to the baton, a change came over him as regards public appearances, and whereas formerly it was only with the greatest difficulty he could be induced to step on to a platform, he accepted invitations to conduct his own works with what in him could almost be termed alacrity, and during the next few years we find him frequently leaving his retirement for Cologne, Dresden and other musical centres in Germany. In 1890 he made a prolonged stay at Florence. Much of his time in these later years, however, was spent at the country house at Frolovskoye which he had acquired in 1888.

Towards the end of the same year Tchaikovsky was much grieved by the gradual cooling of the interest Mme von Meck took in him. Some little while previously he had heard that her financial position was not as brilliant as it had been. She had incurred considerable losses through the extravagance of her eldest son and her income was likely to be considerably reduced. Her alarms subsequently proved to have been exaggerated, but as he himself had reached what in the case of so modest a man was real affluence, the acceptance of the yearly stipend preyed upon his mind, and eventually the arrangement came to an end. Unfortunately, so did their correspondence, which had lasted now close upon fourteen years, and the composer felt deeply hurt that this should be so. On his death-bed, even in the height of fever, the name of Nadezhda Filaretovna was perpetually on his lips. Like most sensitive men, he was prone to dwell upon his grief until it assumed in his mind extraordinary proportions. Mme von Meck was in reality not to blame. Never robust, she had become very delicate in the last few years, and was passing into a decline which led to her death two months after she received the news of that of Peter Ilyich. Her malady was complicated by acute nervous symptoms, and it is probable that physical reasons alone accounted for her allowing her friendship to become dormant. Her second son, Nicholas, married Tchaikovsky's niece. He was a director of the Moscow-Kazan Railway and was shot by order of the Cheka in 1929.

The following year Tchaikovsky paid his only visit to America, where he gave six concerts, four in New York, one in Baltimore and one in Philadelphia. His European success was repeated there, and his praises were sung as only the American press could sing them. Nevertheless, he does not seem to have enjoyed the trip, and in his diary complains occasionally of being treated with contempt at the various hotels he stayed at. Altogether he was in a state of great depression, having heard at Rouen of the death of his sister, Alexandra Davidov, just before he embarked for the U.S.A.

The last two years of his life were full of travel. He had now attained European fame, and his diary and letters record a series of veritable triumphs. This did not, however, prevent a gloomy state of mind from gaining upon him, and there are many who see in this some sinister foreboding of the end. One is always tempted after the event to read significance into facts which do not possess it. For instance, the increased anxiety which he displayed about the publication of his works at this time would seem to imply a presentiment, but is more likely to have been due to a more acute phase of his chronic nervous disorder.

Tchaikovsky's last concert tour, in June 1893, brought him again to England, to receive the degree of Doctor of Music *honoris causa* from the University of Cambridge, which was conferred at the same time on Saint-Saëns, Boito, Max Bruch and Grieg. At the invitation of the Philharmonic Society he conducted his fourth Symphony with such enormous success in London that a renewed visit was arranged for the following year. Had not fate intervened, he would thus have brought the 'Pathetic' Symphony to us in person, but his intention was faithfully carried out by the Society during the season which followed his death. Its success was instantaneous. The Society repeated it by unanimous request, and almost immediately afterwards it passed into the repertory of the Henschel and other symphony concerts. In the second part of this volume will be found an account of the production of this Symphony, which was to be the composer's swan-song. It was performed for the first time on 28th October 1893 at St. Petersburg. Four days later he drank a glass of unfiltered water in a restaurant, and on 6th November he died of cholera.

In Modest Tchaikovsky's book there is a detailed account of the course of the malady which dealt this sudden blow to musical Russia. In a work of such magnitude it was inevitable that this should be included for the sake of completeness, but it would be out of place in a smaller book to dwell upon such matters, when the greater aspect of the tragedy calls us. Tchaikovsky, at the time of his death, was but fifty-three years old—young for a great composer.

TCHAIKOVSKY DURING THE LAST YEARS OF HIS LIFE

CHAPTER VI

THE MAN AND HIS MUSIC

ALTHOUGH certain of Tchaikovsky's earlier works, the *Romeo and Juliet* Overture for example, revealed the touch of a master-hand, one can safely say that it was only within more recent times that, in the phrase dear to the critics, he had found himself, and the last three Symphonies, or better still, the last two, foreshadowed a period of creative enthusiasm of the highest type. His death not only dashed these hopes to the ground, but actually caused a gloom to fall over the entire school of music of which Tchaikovsky was the protagonist. Although it is pleasant to record that for many years previously all friction which had existed between Tchaikovsky and the leaders of the nationalist group had given way to most cordial relations and mutual admiration, there was no actual fusion of the nationalist and eclectic elements, unless perhaps in the person of Glazunov, the youngest of the group, who was a frequent correspondent and companion of Tchaikovsky during the last period of his life.

Apart from its musical side, Tchaikovsky's character and personality were extremely interesting, albeit somewhat baffling to those who did not know him well. Outwardly timid and nervous, he was inwardly capable of great strength, though its exertion in the strong situations of life usually left him afterwards in a state of collapse, and even of dangerous illness. His extreme discomfort whenever brought into contact with strangers, however amiable and flattering their intentions towards him, was so accentuated as to afford a fitting subject for a psychologist; but his mental attitude at the same time was not one of timidity—it would indeed be hard to define it, for neither was there anything offensive about it—but was merely a kind of reserve, which in no way prevented him from forming lasting friendships with those who had thus incommoded him the moment he realized their worth. His actions and letters reveal him as possessing a generous and amiable disposition which would shrink from causing any one a moment of pain. Like many men of this type he was long-suffering, and though his sensitiveness might cause him to wince many times, the offender had a long shrift before Tchaikovsky allowed resentment to get the better of him. When, however, this point had been reached, he could be most unforgiving, though not unjust.

Much has been made of his pessimism, but it is at least open to doubt whether this was personal or racial. In every Slav there lies hidden a fatalist, and, combined with a certain fluidity of emotion, running rapidly over the whole gamut of human joy and sorrow, this fatalism engenders in every true Russian moments of gloom and depression such as we Westerners can little appreciate. That modern sensation for which Germans coined the word *Weltschmerz* has little in common with it.

On the whole, Tchaikovsky's works, with their strong emotions and occasionally violent contrasts, form the most reliable basis for a clear estimate of his character, and even where conclusions formed from them may not strictly correspond with what we know of his life, the wise man will nevertheless give them the preference, for as time goes on, a man's biography pales into insignificance beside the monument he has set himself. Ignorance of Spitta's book never obscured any true musician's love of Bach, and it would be better not to know a single fact of Tchaikovsky's life than not to know his greater creations.

There are two methods of describing in detail the heritage of a great creative artist. These are the chronological method, which reviews his output year by year, and should therefore form a corollary to his biography, if not an integral part of it; and the systematic method, which classifies it under its various headings and sub-headings, and has for its object the convey-ance of an adequate impression of the subject's contributions to any one branch of his art. In the absence of a biography the former plan would commend itself; but the entire career of Tchaikovsky having been traced through its various phases from the historical point of view, to wade once more through nis life, describing how each year was occupied, could only lead to tedious repetition of what has gone before. That is one reason why the systematic plan would appear to be the most applicable to the present purpose. It has, however, many other advantages: for instance, by adopting it the various groups into which Tchaikovsky's works fall may be treated from different points of view.

It is undeniable that in this country Tchaikovsky steps nearer to his admirers as a writer of instrumental, and especially orchestral, music than he does either as a dramatic composer or a song writer. In the latter capacity he has never been justly appreciated. His songs, which rank among the most beautiful that have reached us from a land often described as a land of song, have been kept almost entirely out of our programmes, in which his symphonies have long held sway. His operas, but for a few unsuccessful productions and a thoroughly adequate one of *Eugene Oniegin*, are practically unknown here; nor is there much prospect of their ever obtaining a firm footing, as they belong to a type of dramatic

C

music for which Western audiences have been to a large extent spoiled. Therefore, with a view to giving prominence to those details which are primarily interesting to the concert-going reader, I shall deal exhaustively with Tchaikovsky's instrumental works, less so with his songs, and review his dramatic music principally from the dramatic standpoint: that is to say, in its relation to the stories themselves rather than its musical importance.

On the other hand, I am loath to sacrifice the advantages of the chronological method. In order to follow correctly the musical development of Tchaikovsky, it is imperative that the reader should not only have a concise idea of the manner in which his works group themselves, but also of the period each one belongs to. To this end it will be sufficient to follow the present section of this little volume by a chronology which gives in detail the work upon which Tchaikovsky was engaged during each year of his musical life. By consulting this calendar the reader will be able in a moment to locate the exact period of any composition referred to, and, with the same glance, ascertain with which other compositions it is contemporary. This is eminently desirable, as it obviates the one defect of the proposed systematic review.

The order in which to proceed presents little or no difficulty. After relating in the manner described the composer's various achievements in the dramatic field, one passes almost instinctively to his orchestral music, a great proportion of which is also dramatic in the higher sense. From this to his chamber music and other instrumental works is but a step. In conclusion, we have Tchaikovsky the song writer, not by any means the least great of the Tchaikovskys.

CHAPTER VII

THE OPERAS

TCHAIKOVSKY'S first opera, *The Voyevoda,* is based on a drama by Ostrovsky, who compressed its five acts and prologue into a libretto of three acts only and adapted it to operatic requirements. It is said by those who are acquainted with both the drama and the libretto that the abbreviation necessary in constructing the latter had the effect of robbing the main thread of the story of the beautiful background of subordinate incident which rendered it so attractive in the original form. The libretto was handed to Tchaikovsky early in 1867, but it was then in the experimental stage. The author and the composer found many consultations necessary before it could stand. They collaborated in this sense until about the middle of the second act was reached, from which point the composer appears to have taken the upper hand. It is not on record that there was any acute divergence of opinion between them, although Tchaikovsky's ruthless stripping away of everything he did not fancy must have been rather galling to the poet.

As only the overture and the dances are extant it is impossible to say how far Tchaikovsky succeeded with this first opera. Its production on 11th February 1869 was a remarkable popular success, the composer being recalled no less than fifteen times. Musically speaking, it was probably not so satisfactory. Laroche attacked it in unmistakable terms, and, in spite of

Tchaikovsky's high regard for his opinion, an estrangement was caused between them which lasted over two years. Eventually he must have seen the justice of the criticism, for he destroyed the score himself not many years later. In spite of its unusual success the opera was performed only five times. At a much later date the same subject was treated by Arensky, who, to prevent confusion, called his opera *A Dream on the Volga*, that being the sub-title of Ostrovsky's drama, and Tchaikovsky was large-minded enough to speak in warmest praise of this opera, which he placed on a much higher musical level than his own early and probably immature work.

In recording the destruction of this first opera and its immediate successor *Undine*, we must not lose sight of the fact that Tchaikovsky saw no artistic objection to retaining such material as he thought worthy to survive and subsequently using it for a totally different purpose. Thus there are several parts of *The Voyevoda* incorporated in *The Oprichnik*, whilst fragments of *Undine* are to be found in *Snegourochka*, the second Symphony and the ballet entitled *The Swan Lake*. The composer's genius was, of course, at all times sufficient to enable him to bend his material to his purpose of the moment, but in spite of that one cannot avoid having certain misgivings as to the ultimate appropriateness of the ideas.

Tchaikovsky found the libretto of *Undine* ready to his hand amongst the works of Count Sologub, who as far back as 1848 had constructed it for the composer Lvov on the basis of a poem by Zhukovsky. The story is in itself a pretty one, and the libretto, of which a summary is given in Modest Tchaikovsky's book, reveals distinctly greater possibilities of successful musical handling than *The Voyevoda*. Unfortunately it was never performed. It was rejected in a peremptory and final manner by the authorities of the St. Petersburg opera-house, and beyond a few excerpts which were performed at a concert in March 1870, nothing was heard of it. The recorded opinions were on the whole favourable to these pieces, but the ill-luck which pursued Tchaikovsky in these early days was apparently insurmountable.

In regard to the next subject by which the composer was attracted for dramatic purposes this ill-luck manifested itself in a new form. The libretto of *Mandragora* was full of such palpable absurdities that all his friends, and especially Kashkin, unanimously urged him to desist from the work. With great regret, and in spite of the liking he had for the text, he complied, and only one number saw the light of day. This was the chorus of insects. It is written for the unusual combination of boys singing in unison, accompanied by mixed chorus and orchestra. The realization of the moonlit scene and highly fantastic surroundings is very happy, and Balakirev expressed himself in terms of warmest approval, although he did not forget to point out some rather shadowy indebtedness to Dargomizhsky and Borodin.

No sooner had Tchaikovsky dismissed *Mandragora* from his mind than he was already busy with another subject, a tragedy by Lashetchnikov entitled *The Oprichnik*. This was the name given to the soldiers who formed the bodyguard of the Tsar Ivan the Terrible. The action of the tragedy is very powerful, and moreover lends itself admirably to operatic treatment. Nevertheless the libretto which Tchaikovsky himself compiled from this material was anything but an artistic success. For this there were two strong reasons. First, there was the action of the censor, who would not allow any profane characterization of a Russian Tsar, even though he were Ivan the Terrible, and then there was the composer's determination to drag in all that was worth saving of *The Voyevoda* and find room for it in the first act. Being his own poet, or rather adapter, he did not scruple to transplant passages of the actual text from one opera into the other, so that there was even much of Ostrovsky in the resulting mixture. The excuse he gave for all this was a surprising one: the scene was in both cases the same, namely the courtyard of a castle, therefore it all fitted in beautifully! It does not appear to have struck him that the various personages of his opera were thereby robbed of their musical individuality until the second act, and that three-quarters of an hour after the opening of an opera is a little late to commence musical characterization. However, with all its faults, the libretto contains, at least in its later scenes, some really brilliant situations, and it is not altogether surprising to hear that it was a success when it was produced on 24th April 1874. This success, it is true, did not lead to more than fourteen performances, but this is considerably more than many of the finest Russian operas of those days could boast of—in fact not one of those which were actually contemporary with *The Oprichnik* exceeded the sum total of sixteen performances. Although Tchaikovsky himself did not desire it, nearly all his colleagues from Moscow, with Nicholas Rubinstein at their head, came to St. Petersburg to be present at the first performance, and witnessed his first real operatic success. In a box were Ilya Tchaikovsky and his family, and Modest relates that he pluckily asked the proud father whether this artistic triumph were not really finer than, for example, the order which might have been awarded Peter Ilyich if he had persevered in his official career. But the reply was not encouraging: Ilya had lost none of his affection for the career of a functionary and admitted his preference for an order.

After the performance, the directors of the Musical Society of Moscow and St. Petersburg gave a dinner in the composer's honour, in the course of which he was informed with becoming ceremony that he was to participate, to the extent of three hundred roubles, in a trust fund bequeathed two years previously by a generous amateur for the benefit of young Russian composers.

Tchaikovsky was not slow in realizing the imperfections of *The Oprichnik,* which were pointed out, notably by Cui, with perhaps unnecessary acidity, and in spite of his success he lost all pride in his work within a fortnight of its production. His dissatisfaction was not limited to the libretto, but in course of time the shortcomings of the music became magnified in his imagination, until finally he came to regard the work as an abomination of which he felt utterly ashamed. In his letters he repeatedly gives vent to his dislike of the work, and on one occasion, when the authorities caused it to be withdrawn as being of somewhat too revolutionary a tendency for the times, he congratulated himself most heartily and openly announced his intention of doing all he could to prevent any future performances.

Tchaikovsky's next opera was written for a competition. During the last years of his life the composer Serov became animated by the desire to write a Russian comic opera, and, after much searching, discovered a suitable subject in a short story by Gogol. At that time he was in great favour with the Grand Duchess Helena, and, upon his describing his plan to her, she entered so thoroughly into it that she proposed to have the libretto written for him by Polonsky at her own expense. Unfortunately the death of the composer intervened before he could approach his task. In honour to his memory the grand duchess decided to offer two prizes of one thousand and five hundred roubles respectively for the two best settings of the libretto. There seems to have been a sort of fatality about the poem as, before this plan could be carried out, the grand duchess herself also died, in January 1873; but the Imperial Russian Music Society took the matter over, and after having first approached the principal musical people in Russia, including Tchaikovsky himself, as to the best means of carrying out the grand duchess's scheme, the competition was announced, and Tchaikovsky promptly set to work to compose an opera for it. Thus originated the opera *Vakula the Smith* which, as we shall see, had as varied a career as any of the operas we have hitherto discussed. It marks the close of the earlier and less effective period of Tchaikovsky's dramatic work, whilst the opera which was the next to make its appear-ance represents the opening of an era of operatic successes.

The method by which the libretto of *Vakula* was constructed has been subjected to much criticism. It is often advanced that it would have been more legitimate to confine the attention to the love story of Vakula and Oxana, but, as a matter of fact, to have done so would have called for greater development of that story than the original version of Gogol warranted. Polonsky did not attempt to do anything of the kind, but made his libretto consist of a string of episodes, much as Gogol had done before him. It is true that in the result a certain lack of unity is felt, but this defect is amply compensated for by the charming manner in which the episodes themselves are treated, the attention of the audience being riveted at all times on what is immediately before it, and becoming too deeply interested to trouble about the relative importance of the scene to the main thread. The plan of the opera is worth closer description.

Act I. A moonlit winter landscape in the village of Dikanka. The witch Solokha emerges from her hut to enjoy the moonlight. A demon follows her with his attentions, and they sing a humorous duet, at the end of which they resolve to take a ride through the air. Solokha goes to fetch a broom, and also to rake up the fire, so that she may make a successful ascent of the chimney in a cloud of smoke. During her absence the demon gives vent to his hatred of the witch's son Vakula, the smith, who has chalked his picture on the wall in such a manner that, as he says, all the silly devils laugh with joy. In revenge he conjures up a snowstorm. The witch flies from the chimney on her broom, and the demon follows her and steals the moon, causing darkness to fall. Tchub, Oxana's father, who is on his way home, loses himself in the obscurity, and arrives, without knowing it, at the door of his own cabin. The whole scene is hidden by clouds of snow, which, on clearing, reveal the interior of Tchub's hut. Oxana is alone, whiling away the time with singing and with admiring her own beauty in the looking-glass. Vakula enters and declares his love, but Oxana only laughs at him. During her temporary absence in the next room, her father, Tchub, enters, but Vakula, who has never seen him, mistakes him for an intruder, and throws him out. When Oxana on returning is informed of what has happened, she not un-naturally flares up, and drives Vakula away with a flea in his ear. Left to herself, however, she pities him. Nevertheless she cannot think of him without laughing. In fact, she is in that state, so well known to the fair sex, of not knowing whether to cry or laugh.

Act II. In the witch's hut. Solokha has just returned from her ride on the broomstick and is adjusting her toilet. The demon comes out of the stove to flirt with her, and they dance to music supplied by imps in the shape of crickets and cock-roaches, which appear in all the cracks and crevices of the hut. A knock at the door. The demon hastily conceals himself in a sack. Then follow three similar scenes as the village

*C   63

28278

headman (*golova*), the church deacon (*diak*) and Tchub enter in the same manner, and four sacks are occupied. Vakula follows, and is so deeply concerned with his love affair that he carries the sacks one after the other to the smithy without noticing their weight. The scene changes to a street in the village of Dikanka. The moon has been replaced. The boys and girls, among them Oxana, are singing Christmas carols. On perceiving Vakula, Oxana cannot resist the temptation to tease him again, and tells him that she will never marry him until he brings her the shoes worn by the empress herself. He, absent-mindedly, leaves the heaviest of his sacks behind him, and only removes that containing the demon. After his departure, avowedly to drown himself in his despair, the boys and girls open the sacks, and from them emerge, amidst the wildest merriment, the village headman, the church deacon and Tchub.

Act III. A forest glade near the river. The river fairies under the ice are complaining bitterly of the cold. Vakula enters and drops his sack on the ground, whereupon the demon crawls out and persuades him, rather violently, to sell his soul for the love of Oxana. Obtaining a moment's freedom for the purpose of signing the document, Vakula turns the tables on the demon by seizing him and refusing to liberate him until he has brought him to the empress, and obtained the shoes Oxana has demanded. In the second scene Vakula and the demon arrive in St. Petersburg. The smith mixes with the victorious Cossacks, who are to be presented to the Tsar. Great festivities take place at court, in honour of the Russian victors. During them Vakula approaches the empress and begs for the shoes, which are granted him. The final scene takes place on Christmas morning whilst the people are coming out of the village church. All are joyful except

Solokha, who misses her son, and Oxana, who at last regrets having driven away her lover with her ridicule. Then Vakula returns with the shoes and with presents for Tchub, and all are presumably happy ever after.

The intensely scrappy nature of the above story will not escape the reader, and to most Englishmen its general purport will appear not far removed from nonsense. It is only one who has learned to appreciate the beauties which Russian poets understand so well how to hide in the naïve guise of a fairy story who will see through the chaos and realize what could be done with that material by a great poet and a great composer.

The date fixed for the sending in of the competing operas was 13th August 1875, but by some unaccountable oversight Tchaikovsky was under the impression that it was exactly twelve months earlier, and he worked at a furious pace to get ready in time. When he found that his work was completed and that he would have to wait a year before anything came of it, he was very much upset. Nicholas Rubinstein had spoiled him for waiting by performing most of his works almost before the ink was dry. His anxiety to have *Vakula* produced was the greater that he believed himself able by its means to remove the blot on his escutcheon which he always maintained *The Oprichnik* to be. These circumstances and his woefully guile-less nature account for his remarkable indiscretions in connec-tion with the opera. Long before the date fixed he had talked about his work to all and sundry, totally regardless of the importance of anonymity in any competition, and he had committed himself even further by approaching the manage-ment of the St. Petersburg opera-house with a view to having his work performed there before the award. Naturally he set everybody against him, and had the utmost difficulty in con-vincing even his friends of the entire innocence of his motives.

However, matters were eventually smoothed over. Tchaikovsky's score, copied in a hand not likely to be recognized by
the jury, was sent in and was awarded the prize. Although
the ceremony was performed of opening the envelope bearing
the motto: 'Ars longa, vita brevis,' to ascertain the successful
composer's name, there was never any doubt about it, as, after
taking the trouble to have his score copied, he had written the
motto on it with his own hand in characters which were well
known to every Russian musician. Nevertheless, there can
be no question of any injustice, as we have it on the authority
of more than one member of the jury that it was a case of
Tchaikovsky first and the rest nowhere. Rimsky-Korsakov,
for instance, who was one of the judges, describes the works
sent in as a pitiful commentary on the state of music in Russia.

Tchaikovsky was much encouraged by the rehearsals of his
new opera, in the course of which it met with enthusiastic
approval from all the musical people who were allowed to
attend. Even Cui prophesied a brilliant success. The
management of the theatre spared neither trouble nor expense
in mounting the work. The increase of popularity which had
come to Tchaikovsky since the production of *The Oprichnik*
prompted them to regard the forthcoming performance as a
great event. The composer's disappointment may be imagined
when the opera fell flat. This is generally attributed to the fact
that the audience came with the impression that they were
going to be vastly amused. Their conception of comic opera
was something on the lines of Rossini or Auber, and when
they heard *Vakula* they thought they had been deceived. There
was some applause at the beginning but it gradually fizzled out.
Another fault was, in the eyes of the critics, the tendency
towards a manner of writing too symphonic for the subject. It
was also said that the general character of the music was too

sentimental for comic opera. In spite of these failings the opera was performed seventeen times during the five years following its production on 6th December 1876. Although he never entertained against *Vakula* the same animosity of which *The Oprichnik* was the object, as time went on he found more and more imperfections in it, and it did not surprise his friends when in the autumn of 1884 he decided to rewrite the work. He thereupon also altered its title to that of *Tcherevichki*, or *The Little Shoes*. It is also known, especially out of Russia, as *Oxana's Caprices*. The modification consisted principally in wholesale simplifying. The composer had arrived at the conclusion that he had allowed his care of the musical side of the opera to cause him to lose sight of its decorative and scenic aspect. He considerably lightened the orchestration, and eliminated much of the exaggerated chromaticism of the harmonies. He also added some attractive new numbers, and the entire revision was conducted with such scrupulous care that almost the same audiences which had received the work coldly in its original form became enthusiastic on making its acquaintance in this new garb. It was produced on 31st January 1887.

As already mentioned, the next opera which occupied Tchaikovsky's attention caused him to take the definite leap from incomplete and even questionable local successes to European fame as a dramatic composer. The first mention of this opera occurs in a letter to his brother Modest, dated 30th May 1877. He writes:

I recently called on Madame Lavrovskaya [a famous singer and teacher at the Conservatoire]. The conversation turned on libretti for operas. X—— chattered a lot of nonsense, and made the most ridiculous suggestions. Elizabeth Andreievna [Lavrovskaya] remained silent and merely smiled. Suddenly she remarked: 'How would *Eugene Oniegin* do?' This idea struck me as being very curious, and I made no reply. Later on, however, during a solitary lunch at the restaurant, I remembered *Oniegin*, began to think it over, and found the idea by no means so absurd. A resolution was soon taken, and I at once began to search for Pushkin's works. I had trouble in finding them. A perusal filled me with delight. I spent a sleepless night—result thereof, the scenic scheme of a charming opera with Pushkin's text. No later than the next day I went to Shilovsky, who is now working with lightning speed on my scheme.

He then proceeds to give a short *aperçu* of his plan, and it is interesting to know that in the final version of the opera he made but one solitary departure from his original intentions. The story, as adapted to operatic purposes, and the music set to it, is thus described by Rosa Newmarch in her book on Tchaikovsky:

'The opening scene shows the garden of the Larins' country house. Madame Larin, seated under the trees, is busy preserving her fruit; her daughters, Olga and Tatiana, are seen at the open window of the drawing-room. Their duet, "Hearest thou the Nightingale?" is extremely pretty, in a delicate, sentimental style that seems to carry us back to the days of "sensibility" and clear muslin frocks. After the duet comes a quartet, in which Madame Larin and the old nurse Philipievna take part. Then the peasantry arrive on the scene, and there follows a chorus of harvesters, based on a very original theme, which is quite national in character. At Madame Larin's invitation they start a choral dance. Meanwhile the sisters come into the garden. Tatiana advances dreamily, book in hand, Olga rallies her sister on her romantic proclivities, and sings her first solo, "I have no mind for languor or for sadness," the music of which is in complete contradiction to the words. Their neighbour Lensky, who is in love with Olga, now comes in, and begs permission to introduce his friend Eugene Oniegin. The young men wear high riding-boots and long black cloaks of Byronic fashion. When the young people are left alone, Oniegin entertains Tatiana in a somewhat colourless recitative. After these two have wandered into the garden, Lensky remains with Olga and sings his impassioned love-song, "I love you, Olga." Throughout the entire opera Lensky's music has the most vitality, and is best suited to the character it portrays. Presently the old nurse is sent to announce that tea is served. Her eyes, quickened by love, mark a subtle change in Tatiana. She guesses that her darling has already lost her heart to the "young stranger." As the curtain falls the orchestra, in a few expressive bars, suggests the emotions newly awakened in Tatiana's heart.

'In the second scene of the first act, we see Tatiana's room by moonlight. The nurse comes to remind her that it is bed-time. Then there follows a long, confidential recitative between them, while the orchestra carries on a soft accompaniment based upon Tatiana's *Leitmotiv*. This scene, so exquisite in every detail—and recalling a similar scene in Shakespeare's *Romeo and Juliet*—is deservedly the most popular number in the whole opera. Tatiana's part is a musical *chef-d'œuvre*, and the nurse's tale, told to an air in the style of a Russian folksong, is excellent. When the nurse has departed, Tatiana falls into a reverie, from which she rouses to sing her beautiful little song, "Nay, though I be undone," in which she tells her love of Oniegin. But how will he guess her secret unless she reveals it herself? Then she resolves to write a love-letter to him. Meanwhile, the orchestra delicately indicates all the emotions through which Tatiana is passing. Her modesty, her maidenly misgivings, her despair, her ecstasy, and the final triumph of passionate first love. When the nurse returns, the letter is finished, and Tatiana begs her to convey it to Oniegin. She hesitates, but cannot refuse anything to this child of her heart. As she reluctantly departs on her errand, Tatiana, seated at her writing-table, sinks once more into her dreamy mood, and the curtain falls once more to her characteristic motive.

'The third scene takes us back to the garden of the Larins' house, and opens with a chorus based on a folksong, sung by the peasant girls, who have been gathering berries. As Tatiana enters, the orchestra depicts her ill-concealed agitation. She has not seen the young stranger since she sent her love-letter, and by morning light her conduct seems unmaidenly. Presently Oniegin enters. He cannot appreciate the directness and sweetness of Tatiana's nature. To his jaded mind this simple country-girl is insipid; for he is of the type that finds the savour of love "not in the woman but the chase." He thanks her coldly for her letter, but assures her that he is not a marrying man; and after offering her brotherly affection, gives her some half-cynical advice as to the need of more maidenly reserve in future. Finally he leaves her crushed with shame and the pain of a first disappointment.

'The fourth scene opens upon a brilliantly lighted room in the Larins' house. The guests are dressed in the quaint costumes and uniforms of the twenties. The ball is in honour of Tatiana's birthday. An old-fashioned slow valse is heard in the orchestra. Oniegin, whom Lensky has dragged to the ball against his will, stands apart from the guests in a mood of cynical boredom. He resolves to console himself by flirting with Olga, and carries her off to dance, leaving Lensky—who is now her accepted lover—fuming with jealousy and injured vanity. Oniegin's music in this scene is probably meant to illustrate his condition of mind, but it leaves an impression of weakness, as well as of coldness, which does not accord with his character. The complimentary couplets to Tatiana, sung to an old-fashioned French air by a typical Frenchman, Triquet, make a pleasant break in the continual valse-rhythm which accompanies the first part of this scene. After Triquet's solo, the valse gives place to a mazurka, and Olga is again seen dancing and flirting with Oniegin. Lensky loses his self-control, and unwisely demands an explanation. Oniegin is coldly insolent, and Olga rebellious. Lensky first insults his friend, and then forces a challenge upon him. Oniegin now feels some qualms of conscience, but it is too late to retreat or apologize. He consents to go out with Lensky, and the party breaks up in consternation.

'The fifth scene represents a winter landscape at dawn. The short orchestral prelude is founded on Lensky's *leitmotiv,* one of the most interesting subjects in the opera. While Lensky is awaiting Oniegin's arrival, he sings his aria, "My days of youth, where have they fled?" which is one of the best and most characteristic of Tchaikovsky's inspirations. After the sincere pathos of Lensky's air, the conventional duel scene which follows seems rather poor and stagy.

'Some years are supposed to elapse between the fifth and sixth scenes. The curtain rises upon a reception-room in a luxurious house in St. Petersburg. The guests are seen moving to and fro to the music of a brilliant polonaise. Apart from the rest, Oniegin stands in gloomy reflection. In a long and not very interesting recitative, he tells of his remorse for Lensky's death, his wanderings in search of peace, and of his jaded spirit, which can find no satisfaction in love or folly. Meanwhile the ball goes on, and the guests are all awaiting the arrival of the acknowledged belle of society, the Princess Gremin. She proves to be Tatiana, grown into a gracious

71

and stately woman of the world. Her husband, Prince Gremin, is a dignified nobleman, high in the diplomatic world, middle-aged but handsome, and devoted to his beautiful young wife. Oniegin is astonished to recognize in this dazzling woman the girl whose love he had rejected. His chilly egoism is thawed, and he falls passionately in love.

'The last scene takes place in the boudoir of Princess Gremin. She is reading a letter from Oniegin. Tatiana has been quietly happy with her elderly prince, but the sight of her first love has awakened her stronger emotions. His letter throws her into a state of agitation, and before she can recover her self-control, Oniegin bursts in upon her with a passionate declaration of love. In a long duet, in which the emotion is kept at extreme tension, Oniegin implores her to have pity and to fly with him, while she struggles between honour and reawakened love. Finally, with a supreme effort, she breaks away from him at the very moment when she has just confessed her true feeling. When the curtain falls, Oniegin, baffled and despairing, is left alone on the stage.'

The libretto consists almost entirely of unaltered lines selected from Pushkin's text, and only in rare instances, where a deviation was absolutely necessary, was foreign matter interpolated. For this Tchaikovsky himself was mainly responsible, the collaboration of Shilovsky being limited to some almost insignificant portions. Nevertheless, the libretto does not impress one favourably. It is rather patchy, and the music itself does not maintain an equally high level throughout; but there is something so eminently lovable about the entire conception, that the picking of flaws becomes an ungrateful task. The popularity of this opera is by no means limited to Russia. It has been performed with success in many parts of the Continent, notably at Vienna, where it has attracted large audiences, but this success is due in a much greater degree to the sympathetic characters and their no less sympathetic treatment than to any overwhelming artistic interest. As a matter of fact, the opera contains many missed opportunities. The musical characterization is far from well defined, and the music allotted to each part lacks contrast. The beauty revealed throughout is rather of a physical type, and it is not surprising to read that Berezevsky describes the opera as being like a woman with many faults of heart and character, but whom we love for her beauty in spite of them all. It has recently been added to the repertory of the Vic.-Wells Opera in London.

The second scene of the first act was composed by 18th June 1877, and on the 27th of the same month the first act was completed. Two-thirds of the work was finished by 5th July, but then the composer rested for a month. The opera was completed at Kamenka in August, but the orchestration occupied him from time to time until the following January. The first performance of the opera took place at the little theatre of the Moscow Conservatoire, where it was produced by the students on 29th March 1879. The circumstances are best described in Tchaikovsky's own words contained in a letter to Mme von Meck, dated two days afterwards:

I have just returned from Moscow. Instead of going there on Friday, I travelled on Wednesday, because Jurgenson had wired me that my presence during the last rehearsal would be desirable. I arrived in Moscow just before the beginning of the rehearsal. It was taking place with the stage well lighted, and in costume, whereas the hall was in darkness. That enabled me to find a seat in a dark corner and hear the whole of my opera uninterrupted. The performance was, generally speaking, satisfactory. Chorus and orchestra did their share excellently, but the solos left much to be desired.

These hours spent in a dark corner of the theatre were the only pleasant ones of my stay in Moscow. In the intervals I saw all my former colleagues again. I rejoiced to observe that they had all taken a great liking for the music of *Oniegin*. Nikolai Gregorievich [Rubinstein], who is so sparing of praise, told me he had fallen in love with this music. Taneiev tried after the first act to express his sympathy to me, but broke into tears. I can hardly tell you how much that affected me. On the Saturday, the day of the performance, my brothers arrived and also some people from St. Petersburg, among them Anton Rubinstein.

I was very excited all day, especially when I had given way to the urgent request of Nikolai Gregorievich and declared my readiness to appear on the stage, should I be called for.

During the performance my excitement reached the highest limit. Before the commencement, Nikolai Gregorievich had asked me on to the stage, where, to my terror, I saw the entire Conservatoire. At the head of the professors stood Nikolai Gregorievich, who handed me a wreath, whilst everybody applauded. Naturally, I had to reply with a few words to Rubinstein's address—what that cost me, Heaven alone knows! In the intervals I was called many times. Still, it did not appear that any great delight was felt among the public. I gather this from the fact that each time it was I alone, and not the performers, who was called for.

It was only by degrees that Tchaikovsky came to see any future at all for his opera. At first he thought of it merely as pleasant lyrical scenes, which might become popular in the shape of separate numbers, but did not present great possibilities for the stage. Eventually, however, he became convinced of its value, and for once he did not allow himself to be depressed by any lukewarm approval. Such was, for instance, the attitude of Anton Rubinstein, who, without exactly condemning the work, took great pains on his return to St. Petersburg to point out all its faults. Some years later, however, his wife happened to make some similar disparaging remarks about it in his presence, which was quite another thing. He exclaimed: 'What do you know about it? Those who have grown up amidst gipsy tales and Italian operas have no business to talk about such works.'

The composition of Tchaikovsky's next opera, *Joan of Arc*, was begun at Clarens in January 1879 and finished at Simaki the following August. The libretto was his own, although largely based on Zhukovsky's Russian translation of Schiller's *Maid of Orleans*. At the outset he was disposed to keep entirely to this version, but he could not reconcile himself to the great German poet's frequent acts of disrespect towards historical facts. Neither did the ending of Schiller's drama please him. He himself owns to being further indebted to a book on the subject by Wallon, a drama by Barbier and the libretto of an opera by Mermet.[1] The compiling of this text, to judge by the references to it in his correspondence, gave him no end of trouble. He complained frequently of the difficulty of finding rhymes and cried aloud for a rhyming dictionary, which does not appear to have existed in Russia at that date. In one letter he hints at the number of splintered pen-holders represented by every few lines of his text. Shortly before his death he had decided to remodel the close of his opera in the sense of bringing it into line with the close of Schiller's tragedy, but his sudden and fatal illness overtook him before he was ready to begin the revision.

Although the story of the great French heroine is so well known, and Schiller's fine play almost equally so, the subject itself seems so remote from operatic treatment that it will scarcely be deemed out of place if a full synopsis of the method

[1] Auguste Mermet (1810–89). His *Jeanne d'Arc* (1876) was the first new production in the present Paris Opéra.

adopted is given here. This was communicated by Tchaikovsky in a letter to his brother Modest.

Act I. Village maidens are decorating an oak tree with flowers and singing. Enter Thibaut, Joan's father, and Raymond, who is courting her. Thibaut says that it is not the time to sing and play, as the country is threatened with danger. It would be best for a woman to have a male defender at her side, and therefore he wishes Joan to be betrothed to Raymond. She is silent. At length she says that she is destined for another fate. Thibaut is angry; he suspects her of dealings with evil spirits, and overwhelms her with reproaches. On the horizon one sees the reflection of fire, and the alarm bell is heard. By degrees the scene is filled with fugitive peasants, who have been robbed of their all by the English, and are seeking refuge. Thibaut asks what has become of the king's army. Old Bertrand describes the despairing situation of the country. All are appalled; Orleans is besieged by the invincible Salisbury. Suddenly Joan steps forward with inspiration, declares that the end of these misfortunes is come, and prophesies the triumph of France. The crowd is astonished and does not believe her: 'Ours is not the time of miracles.' Joan exclaims: 'Yes! the miracle has already happened; Salisbury is killed.' None believes her. Thibaut is convinced that she is in league with the devil. A soldier arrives from Orleans and bears witness that Salisbury is really dead. Then they all believe Joan and kneel to pray. The crowd having dispersed, Joan says that the time has come to act; she is overcome with grief at leaving her home, the sound of the village church bells brings her to the verge of despair, but suddenly a chorus of angels is heard saying that the day has come. She implores that this cup may be allowed to pass her by, but the angels encourage her and she becomes determined, passing into a state of ecstasy, and uttering words of wisdom.

Act II. The castle of Chinon. The king is sitting deep in thought, with Dunois and Agnes, listening to the music of minstrels. When they have concluded he orders that they shall be entertained, and that each one shall receive a gold chain. Dunois observes that chains cannot be made out of words, and that the treasury is empty. Agnes declares that such being the case it is every one's duty to give everything for the army. She disappears to collect her jewels. The king looks after her and says that misfortune is easily borne when one is loved by such a woman. Dunois urges the king to advance at the head of his army for the defence of France The king is not averse, but cannot bring himself to part with Agnes. A wounded knight enters, accompanied by some warriors, and brings the news that the battle is lost, and that the king must either fly or perish on the field of honour. He expires at the king's feet. The king loses courage, and thinks of flight. Dunois indignantly leaves him, and he remains alone in dull despair. Agnes returns, bringing her jewel casket, and the king tells her what has happened. She is terrified, but endeavours to console him, and sings to him of her love. Fanfares are heard, and the stage is gradually filled. Dunois enters and announces that a miracle has happened, and that the victory has been snatched from the English. The king is incredulous, but the archbishop enters and confirms the news, describing how in the most critical moment a maiden appeared and put the English to flight. One hears the shout of the people and the joyful ringing of bells. Joan enters, surrounded by knights. Previously to this the king has motioned Dunois to the royal throne and disappeared into the crowd of courtiers; but Joan is not to be deceived, and promptly finds the king.

He is astonished. She thereupon tells him the purport of his last three prayers. This convinces the king and all bystanders. Asked who she is, she narrates her story. All are moved to tears, but their emotion gives way to enthusiasm as the king places Joan at the head of his army amidst acclamations.

Act III. Scene i. Field in the neighbourhood of Rheims. Meeting of Joan with Lionel. They fight; she overcomes him and forces him to yield his sword. In this moment she sees his face, and they fall in love with each other. She begs him to fly, as her followers are coming, but he refuses to leave her. Dunois appears, and Lionel informs him that he wishes to go over to the French army. Dunois rejoices that France has won so great a captain, and welcomes him in the name of the king. Joan faints from the effect of a wound. Scene ii. Coronation. The king announces to his people that Joan is the saviour of France. Old Thibaut enters and declares that it is not by the aid of heaven, but with help from hell that Joan has been victorious. None believes him. Dunois and Lionel are ready to fight in defence of her innocence. Her father leaves her to answer, and she is silent. The archbishop asks her three times if she is pure. She believes herself to be a sinner, and does not reply. All move away from her. Lionel approaches her and says: 'All have left you, but I will remain faithful.' She replies with bitterness that he is her worst enemy, and hastens away.

Act IV. Scene i. A forest. Joan is followed by Lionel. At first she threatens and reviles him, but she is overcome by her own passion, and forgets everything in her love. The fanfares of the English are heard, recalling her to actualities, and she curses both her lover and herself. The chorus of angels sings that the curse of heaven will not fall upon her, although she has not fulfilled its conditions, and has allowed her heart to open itself to earthly love, thereby being rendered unfit to bring her work to its conclusion. She is exhorted to resign herself now without complaint to her unfortunate fate, in the hope of the reward of immortal blessedness. The English come nearer and nearer. In spite of Lionel's entreaties, Joan will not flee. The English appear on the scene, take her prisoner, and kill Lionel. Scene ii. Rouen. Joan is led to the stake. The crowd is touched and attempts to prevent the execution. Joan loses her courage for a moment, but the chorus of angels brings consolation. She is tied to the stake; a priest holds a wooden cross before her, and the pile is fired.

When the opera was first produced in St. Petersburg on 25th February 1881, the part was allotted to a mezzo-soprano, which circumstance rendered some modifications necessary; but these were only used by this singer, all others adhering to the original version. On the other hand, certain minor altera-tions were introduced a year or so later on the advice of Napravnik. Even before the first performance, the latter had deemed it his duty to point out a host of smaller imperfections which the composer, with unlimited faith in the great experience of the conductor, proceeded to remove, although, surrounded as he was by the intrigues of rival prima donnas, the bickerings of opposed schools of criticism, and other amenities of public life, the labour of revision must have been a sore trial to him.

The performance was a great popular success, amounting to an ovation. Fortunately for himself, the composer left St. Petersburg before he had had time to read the criticisms. It was not until some time later that he became aware of the unusual unanimity with which they damned the work. With very few exceptions, they regarded it as a reactionary and unwholesome blend of the Italians and Meyerbeer, with occasional glimpses of greatly impoverished Russian fantasy.

The leader was of course Cui—it was a position he seldom vacated when the instrumental works of Tchaikovsky were discussed, and never when an opera was produced. His opinion was that it was the weakest work Tchaikovsky had hitherto produced. This can, however, with safety be disregarded, as with Cui the last produced work by Tchaikovsky was always the weakest. Berezovsky regards it, on the other hand, as one of the most brilliant of Tchaikovsky's creations, but his judgment is frequently impaired by his no doubt very excellent emotions. The truth lies midway. The general style of the opera is uneven. There are portions of it which are distinctly in the old conventional operatic manner; there are arias, duets and concerted pieces *à la* Verdi; there are occasionally traits of realism and modernity suggesting in a vague way a Mussorgsky equipped with an orthodox technique; there is also some good tone painting, but the elements do not mix. There is something for each section of the audience, but those appealed to by one portion of the work are frequently repelled by another. Isolated numbers, such as are occasionally heard in the concert room, verge on the magnificent, but it is doubtful whether the work will live in its complete form.

The first sketches for Tchaikovsky's following opera, *Mazeppa,* were probably made during the early part of 1881, but they were made without a real conviction that they would ever be fully developed. In October of that year he admits in a letter to his brother Anatol that the subject does not please him, and does not arouse the slightest enthusiasm. However, the satisfaction he derived from a few scenes with which—a rare thing for him—he was satisfied from the moment they were written, changed his attitude towards this opera, and the following spring found him hard at work at Kamenka, without a trace of that early diffidence, and only troubled because of the noise that went on outside his window. By the middle of July he had completed two acts of the opera, and in September it was finished. Then a new trouble began. The orchestration did not proceed as quickly as he wanted it to, and then the old doubts as to the vitality of his powers returned to him and made the task seem heavier than it can possibly have been to so consummate a master of orchestration. It was not until the spring of 1883 that the work could be handed over to Jurgenson for publication, and the event has some interest, as it occasioned the only recorded difference of opinion between composer and publisher as to terms. There are numberless letters in existence where Tchaikovsky protests energetically against Jurgenson allowing his personal friendship to cause him to behave with unbusinesslike generosity. For once in a way, there is one where the composer protests against being credited too little, principally because the fee suggested was no greater than that he had received for the *Joan of Arc* four years previously, and he considered that some account should be taken of his musical progress in the meantime. This opera was predestined to lead to discussions of this kind. When the production was being arranged for, the administration of the theatre quite seriously proposed a lower figure for the performing rights, on the ground that it consisted of three acts, whereas the rule was four. Naturally Tchaikovsky pointed out that it would have been quite as easy for him to divide it into ten, had he known that the circumstance carried any weight with them; but as the opera not only filled the evening programme, but was logically constructed in the form he had given it, he could not see the point of their objection. The rehearsals began on 27th January 1884, and the first performance took place on 15th February at the Moscow opera-house, being followed three days later by a performance at St. Petersburg. Again the composer was disappointed with the reception of his latest opera. The audience at Moscow was cordial enough, but he attributed this entirely to the local popularity of those concerned in the production, including the principal artists and himself, and not to the merits of the work. Subsequent events seem to have justified this, for *Mazeppa* was only kept in the repertoire during two seasons. Once more Cui, who had doubted the possibility of Tchaikovsky writing a worse opera than *Joan of Arc,* declared that he had succeeded in doing so. The ultimate failure of the opera can largely be ascribed to the faults of the libretto, which, although taken from a well-known poem by Pushkin, entitled *Poltava,* is the work of quite a number of collaborators, each of whom appears to have worked with the principal object of securing the introduction into the opera of his own favourite episode or episodes. In other words, the scenic scheme is overcrowded with dramatic situations resembling each other in their appalling gloominess. As regards the music, it must be remembered that Tchaikovsky, despite what is occasionally written about him out of Russia, was never in the principal sense of the word a nationalist composer. He was rarely at his best when setting out deliberately to write 'Russian' music. The whole of the Malo-Russian local colour demanded by the plot of the opera is clumsily and unconvincingly introduced. His Cossacks are not Cossacks at all, unless perhaps they are Cossacks returning from a continental tour, including a visit to Italy. The only point at which the Russian element is successfully used is the symphonic *entr'acte* entitled *The Battle of Poltava,* which has been frequently heard at Queen's Hall under Sir Henry Wood. This is based mainly on folksongs, of which the principal one is the 'Slava,' the first musical use of which dates as far back as Beethoven, who introduced it into one of the Razumovsky Quartets.

Another feature which militated against a success in the popular sense is the divergence between Pushkin's character of Mazeppa and the more popular conception of the Cossack chief. As a legendary hero he is one thing, in history he is another, and the great Russian poet, in making him a crafty and unscrupulous soldier of fortune, gave history the preference, but it is not always safe to rob a heroic figure of the unearned halo of romance due to tradition. The main thread of the story as told in the opera is the feud between Mazeppa and Kochubey. This originates in the latter's refusal of his daughter's hand, on which Mazeppa, notwithstanding his position as a guest in the house, elopes with her. In the second act Mazeppa, himself the wrongdoer, wreaks vengeance on Kochubey, whom he has captured, and who is tortured and executed. The sensational realism of this act tends to make it almost repulsive, although the inspiration throughout is of the highest order. The third act culminates in the despair of Kochoubey's daughter, whose reason is destroyed by her great grief.

As I have observed, the music wrought round this sombre scheme is at certain moments inspired, but the high level then reached is not maintained, and again a lack of unity in style is to be regretted. There are Italian influences which blend badly with the Russian local colour, and, taken as a whole, the opera is neither Russian nor Italian nor German, nor is it entirely individual, but an unhappy combination of these several elements.

After *Mazeppa*, Tchaikovsky's principal operatic work was the remodelling of *Vakula the Smith*, which has already been referred to; but in January 1885 his attention was drawn to a drama of Shpashinsky, entitled *The Sorceress,* which he read and was favourably impressed by. In reply to his application to the author for permission to use the subject, the latter expressed his great pleasure in making the composer's acquaint- ance, and undertook to write a libretto for him.

There is very little mention in any of the numerous books dealing with Tchaikovsky's life of the progress of the composi- tion in its earlier stages, but the dates have more recently become available. He started upon the opera at the beginning of September 1885, and a great part of the first act was com- pleted early in October. He finished the second act by the end of January 1886 and then, being in low spirits, did nothing more until June. The piano score was completed on 30th August. Work on the opera was then suspended during the composition of the twelve Songs, Op. 60. The orchestration of *The Sorceress* was begun on 5th October and continued through October and November. The opera was produced at St. Petersburg on 1st November 1887. It was received very badly. The public seemed quite indifferent, but the composer does not appear to have realized this at the time, and he subsequently attributed the failure of the opera to the spitefulness of the critics, who, as it happens, do not on this occasion appear to have used such biting terms of con- demnation as were applied to several of his previous operas. After this first performance he introduced several modifications, and on 14th February 1890 the revised opera was performed for the first time in Moscow, but it remained a dead failure, and even the composer's friends make little claim for its merits. The most favourable critic is Ivan Knorr, who speaks with enthusiasm particularly of the first act, an inspired picture of Russian popular life. He points out as the chief fault of the opera a tendency on the composer's part to extend his ideas in accordance with the requirements of musical form, thereby causing the action to drag. He, like the composer's brother, claims that the music has not yet received justice, and a perusal of the reports of its few performances certainly gives one the impression that the execution must have been very poor.

After *The Sorceress* Tchaikovsky returned to his beloved Pushkin for another subject, and chose *The Queen of Spades,* which he began to set in January 1890. His diary contains an entry to the effect that the beginning is plagiarized from Napravnik, but the latter professed to be absolutely unable to discover to which of his works it possesses this alleged resemblance. Most of this opera appears to have been composed during the visit to Italy, of which the string Sextet is a souvenir. It also seems to have caused him fewer misgivings than any of its predecessors, as it was not only completed in a few months, but actually produced before the end of the year —on 19th December—a rapidity of composition which one frequently finds in the composer's instrumental works, but very rarely when he was engaged on an opera.

The libretto of *The Queen of Spades* was written by Modest Tchaikovsky on the basis of a story by Pushkin, bearing the same name. Briefly told, the original plot is as follows:

Hermann, a poor officer, is tortured by a morbid craving for riches. He is told that an old countess, whose niece he loves, possesses the secret of the three lucky cards. Should she, however, divulge it, she is doomed to die. Hermann breaks into the house, and so terrifies the old lady that she dies of fright without having revealed the secret, but afterwards her spirit appears to the young officer, and informs him which cards are the three talismans. Armed with this knowledge, he wins a fortune at the tables by means of the first two cards, but at the third game, the ace of hearts suddenly changes before his very eyes into the queen of spades, and the spirit reappears to mock him.

It is obvious that the subject, in spite of its promising situations, was scarcely rich enough to provide the basis of an opera, and the author of the libretto was under the circum-stances quite justified in weaving into the text episodes rendered necessary for the purpose of providing contrast. As we are now dealing with what after *Eugene Oniegin* is the most suc-cessful of Tchaikovsky's operas, it will not be out of place if the scenic basis of the work is given in the author's own words.

Act I. Scene i. A public garden in spring. Children playing and chorus of nursemaids, etc. Entrance of some of the gilded youth of St. Petersburg, narrating Hermann's passion for cards, and describing how he spends entire nights in the gambling-hells, watching the play without joining in, because he is too poor. Enter Hermann and Tomsky. The former speaks of his love for a noble young lady whose name he does not know, but whom he often meets in the street in company with an old and uncanny-looking dame. They are joined by Prince Yeletzky, who informs them that he is betrothed. Asked who the bride-elect is, he indicates a young lady who is just approaching and turns out to be Hermann's unknown love. The latter is filled with sorrow at the thought that his poverty will part him for ever from his love. Charmed as he is by the sight of Lisa, the enigmatic figure of the duenna awakens a certain fear in him. After the departure of the ladies, Tomsky informs him that there is a legend according to which the old countess knows three cards by backing which it is possible always to win. In his morbid fancy Hermann imagines himself to be destined by fate to obtain this secret at the price of the countess's life, become suddenly rich, and thus be enabled to approach the object of his love. An approaching storm increases his excitement and unbalances his mind, until he believes himself capable of a murder. He resolves to end his life, but determines beforehand to see Lisa at least once and confess his love to her. Scene ii. Lisa and her friends are singing, but the appearance of a prim and strict governess interrupts their merriment, and they disperse, leaving Lisa alone. She does not love her betrothed. Her fancy and her heart are full of the mysterious and gloomy stranger whom she has often met in the street and seen this very day in the gardens. Suddenly Hermann stands before her. She is frightened, but he reassures her and begs her to listen to him, threatening to kill himself then and there if she refuses him a hearing. Terrified but happy at the same time to see the man she loves, she cannot resist the temptation to hear him declare his passion. She, however, plucks up courage to send him away, but at that moment the countess unexpectedly enters, attracted by the noise. Instead of sending Hermann away, Lisa conceals him. The appearance of the old lady reminds Hermann of his morbid fixed idea as to the three cards. Lisa calms the countess and accompanies her from the room. Then she returns, and with a peremptory gesture orders Hermann to go, but he has seen the power of his love and remains.

Act II. Scene iii. A fancy dress ball at the house of an official at the time of the Empress Catherine. The guests are dancing. Enter Lisa and Prince Yeletzky. The prince makes love to her but is coldly received. Amongst the dancers is Hermann. His friends, who know of his hallucinations concerning the three cards, mock him about them and whisper mysteriously amongst themselves. The sight of the countess, who is also present, throws him into a state of mad desire for the secret, and he determines to become possessed of it. Now that he has won Lisa's heart it is not difficult for him to obtain admission to the house. The hosts have, in accordance with the custom of those days, arranged an interlude for the entertainment of their guests. Whilst the attention of all is thus taken up, Hermann begs Lisa for a private interview the same evening. Lisa, who already considers Hermann as her betrothed husband, tells him how he can reach her room, and he disappears in order to discover that of the countess. After his departure the majordomo enters and makes, amid great rejoicing, the announcement that the empress is expected. There is a hurried movement on the part of the guests, and at the moment when the empress is to appear the curtain falls. Scene iv. The countess's room. Hermann enters by a secret door. Hearing steps approaching he conceals himself. The old countess returns from the ball and passes into her boudoir, where her maids prepare her for the night. Lisa also passes through the room and takes one of the maids into her confidence about her rendezvous. The countess returns in her night attire, followed by a number of maids. She is tired, cross and dissatisfied with the ball, declares that in the days of her youth everything was much finer and sings a melody of the old days. Then she sends her attendants away, and gently humming the same tune, dozes off. Hermann awakens her. (At this point the scene is almost identical with Pushkin, even the prose being adhered to and only altered where absolutely necessary.) The old lady is dumb with fright at the sight of the intruder, and dies without disclosing the secret. Lisa is attracted by the noise. The excitement has driven Hermann to the verge of madness, and he tells Lisa of his attempt to ascertain the cards. Lisa is terrified, and cannot free her mind from the suspicion that it is only to gain assistance in his treacherous plans that Hermann has striven to gain her love.

Act III. Scene v. An evening in barracks. Hermann is tortured by visions of the burial of the countess. He cannot free himself from the hallucination that he hears the funeral bell tolling. He imagines that he has stood by the countess's coffin and that she has nodded to him. In the stillness of the night and the darkness of the barracks, an insurmountable fear overcomes him; he attempts to fly, but on the threshold appears the spirit of the countess, who tells him what the cards are. Scene vi. The quay of the Neva in winter. Lisa awaits Hermann, with whom she has a rendezvous. She cannot yet believe that it is only for the sake of the three cards that he has courted her. If he does not appear before midnight she will know that her suspicion was well founded, and that she has been sacrificed to treachery. Twelve o'clock strikes, and he is not there. She is in despair, but suddenly he appears, and on meeting him she forgives all. He also forgets everything, and thinks only of his love; but his madness soon asserts itself again, and he babbles of the three cards and of the gambling-hells. He no longer recognizes Lisa, and hastens away, and the abandoned girl throws herself into the water. Scene vii. A card room. The gambling is in full swing. Tomsky sings the song by Dershavin which Pushkin has taken as the motto of his story. Among the gamblers is also Prince Yeletzky. Hermann appears, and backs successively the first two of the fateful cards. He wins each time. With the third card he is to win a fortune, but the others retire from the game except Yeletzky, who faces him. Instead of the ace he intends to back, he backs by mistake the queen of spades, and loses all he has yet won. The spirit of the countess reappears, and in mad despair Hermann stabs himself.

This conclusion differs from that of Pushkin, which is dry and ironic, but not tragic. Hermann does not commit suicide, but goes mad and is confined in an asylum, where he keeps muttering: 'Three, seven, ace! Three, seven, queen!'

I have already coupled this opera with *Eugene Oniegin* as the most successful of Tchaikovsky's dramatic works. There is another reason for bracketing them. The music is very similar throughout. Many of the most attractive features belong to the interpolated episodes, such as, for instance, the interlude at the ball, which takes the form of a pastoral in which is introduced a charming duet in the style of Mozart. The scene of the countess retiring to sleep is also very effective. The melody she sings, in memory of the days of her youth, is an arietta from Grétry's opera *Richard Cœur-de-Lion*. It is amusing to recall that when the opera was presented by Vladimir Rosing at the London Opera House, a certain critic who shall be nameless singled out this song as being the one bit of real Tchaikovsky melody in the whole opera!

It is said that some of the material of this opera was originally intended for another libretto, also derived from Pushkin, and which Tchaikovsky for some reason or other discarded, but if such be the case the composer has succeeded in removing the traces of the adaptation.

Tchaikovsky's next opera, the last he was to write, was again set to a libretto by his brother Modest. It is a lyrical opera in one act, based on the drama *King René's Daughter*, by the Danish poet Hendrik Herz, and entitled *Iolanthe*. It was composed during the year 1891 and produced on 17th December 1892, the same evening which saw the first performance of the *Casse-Noisette* ballet. The critics, who gave the most contradictory opinions about the ballet, were unanimous about *Iolanthe*—in its disfavour. Modest Tchaikovsky attributes its failure, which in this case appears to have been an irredeemable one, entirely to his own libretto, which he describes as being far too prolix, and in spite of a certain poetic beauty, devoid of real scenic interest. True enough, the music does not possess the quality of holding the attention, notwithstanding its grace and charm, but it contains at least one gem of characterization. The part of the Arab physician called to prescribe for Iolanthe is handled in the most masterly manner, with just sufficient orientalism to make it attractive without imparting unnecessary gaudiness to the music.

We have now concluded our review of Tchaikovsky's operas. The most ardent Tchaikovsky lover can hardly wax enthusiastic about their prospects of immortality. Only two, *Eugene Oniegin* and *The Queen of Spades,* have achieved a real success. It is claimed that the day of *Mazeppa* and *Joan of Arc,* and even perhaps of *The Sorceress,* will come when they are better understood, but if the remarkable popularity of Tchaikovsky in his later years was insufficient to ensure their acceptance by the Russian public, one may be pardoned a certain scepticism as to the future. It was undoubtedly his great ambition to excel in this branch of art, but it is evident from his own writings that he never succeeded in reaching the level of perfection he had set himself as a goal. Like the majority of his compatriots he adhered to the old Italian operatic forms. Possibly his intense love of Mozart may be the primary cause of this attitude, but it must not be forgotten that this affection was shared also by Wagner, and the great German reformer does not appear to have been unduly hampered by it. It is difficult for us to understand on what grounds Tchaikovsky, who had, for instance, a great admiration for Verdi, remained more than frigid when confronted with the *Ring.* Wagnerism at that date had almost become an axiom. Not so in Russia. With the exception of Serov, who attempted occasionally to follow in Wagner's footsteps, the Russian composers of both

schools, nationalists and eclectics, have written operas consisting of arias, stanzas, duets, dances and choral numbers in
the time-honoured style. One result of this is that whereas
even Tchaikovsky's warmest admirers did not foresee a great
future for his operas as such, the facility with which they
divide themselves into separate numbers renders the inclusion
of excerpts in concert programmes an easy matter. They
have made their appearance, for instance, at the Queen's
Hall Promenade Concerts, where excerpts from many of them
have been heard. The cordial reception they have met with
leads us to hope that it will become a practice to give some of
the best scenes of these operas in the concert-room. This is
especially to be desired when a so-called 'Tchaikovsky
evening' is announced.

Incidentally it must be mentioned that through all his life
Tchaikovsky was animated by an intense desire to write an
opera on the subject of Romeo and Juliet, which he considered
almost the highest ideal for a libretto. It is not on record what
circumstance prevented him from approaching the subject,
but possibly he may have been deterred by the existence of
operas on the same text, one of which, at least, enjoys a popularity likely to be dangerous to any future composer approaching
it. The existence of a duet for soprano and tenor, which was
found amongst his manuscripts after his death, may perhaps be
taken as pointing to his having overcome this objection, but
nothing definite has been ascertained on the subject.

CHAPTER VIII

INCIDENTAL MUSIC AND BALLETS

TCHAIKOVSKY'S dramatic works include, besides his operas, some incidental music and three ballets. Commencing with the form which is by its nature more intimately connected with the operatic style, we come to one of the most charming of his early works, viz. the music for a fairy tale by Ostrovsky, entitled *Snegourotchka* (*The Snow Maiden*). It consists of an introduction and eighteen numbers, of which no fewer than twelve are vocal. Tchaikovsky was so much in love with the subject that he wished eventually to make an opera of it, but he delayed so long carrying this intention into effect that he was forestalled by another Russian composer, Rimsky-Korsakov, whose *Snegourotchka* is at the same time one of the most delightful and one of the most popular of all modern Russian operas. He was so upset by this disappointment that for a long time he would have nothing to do with Korsakov's works. It was not until many years later that the score came into his hands, and then he atoned for the past by developing a pronounced affection for it. Kashkin's description of the occasion for which Tchaikovsky's incidental music was written is so happy that I cannot do better than quote it:

The three weeks during which Tchaikovsky was working at the music of *Snegourotchka* were a happy time with him. In the year 1873 the smaller theatre was renovated, and whilst the work was proceeding the three companies, opera, ballet and dramatic, gave their performances in the larger theatre. If I am not mistaken, it was then in the charge of V. P. Begitchev, who hit upon the idea of producing on the big stage a kind of fairy piece, in which all three companies should take part. Ostrovsky was approached with the proposition that he should write such a piece, and the music was entrusted to Tchaikovsky. Ostrovsky chose for his theme the tale of the Snow Maiden and set to work with great ardour. He wrote very quickly, and Peter Ilyich, who had to receive the text from him, had little time, so that he had to hurry in order to keep pace with Ostrovsky. The first messages of spring were appearing in the country, and the approach of this beautiful season always filled Peter Ilyich with delight and poetic inspiration: he loved especially the Russian spring, when nature suddenly awakes from her long winter sleep and sometimes within a few days transforms the whole landscape. The spring of 1873 came, I believe, rather early, so that the writing of the music for the *Spring Fairy Tale* coincided with beginning of spring. Peter Ilyich worked with great enthusiasm, and as there was occasion for haste, he went against his custom inasmuch as he drew upon his evenings. Thus the score, which is of some dimensions, was completed in three weeks without Peter Ilyich having been guilty of any irregularity in his lessons at the Conservatoire. When one considers that these lessons amounted to twenty-seven hours a week, the rapidity with which *Snegourotchka* was composed is absolutely astounding. The first performance took place on 11th [23rd] May, and the greatest effect was reached in the scene of Koupava with King Berendey, which was recited by Mme Nikulina and M. Samarin in splendid style, whilst the orchestra played the magnificent music set to it. The talented and beautiful Kadmina, who had undertaken the rôle of the shepherd Lell, was delightful in her singing and acting. The staging of the piece was, according to the ideas of those days, gorgeous, and cost fifteen thousand roubles. In spite of the excellent rendering, *Snegourotchka* did not have a great success. The paucity of scenic action did not allow any genuine enthusiasm to make itself felt in the audience. On the contrary, a certain coldness was displayed, although some moments were quite charming and did not miss their effect. Ostrovsky was not present at the first performance, having already left for his country house in the government of Kostroma, whither a telegram was sent him after the production.

Soon after this, we professors of the Conservatoire made a trip into the country with Samarin and Mme Kadmina. We went to the so-called 'Sparrow Hill' near Moscow. It was a lovely spring day; the gardens on the hills glowed in their garment of white blossoms, and we were all, under the combined influence of spring and *Snegourotchka*, in a very happy mood. We picnicked out there in the meadows and were soon surrounded by peasants, who stared with great curiosity at the gentry refreshing themselves. It then occurred to Rubinstein to organize a little popular festivity; he went to the village shop and purchased wine and all kinds of sweetmeats, which he distributed amongst those present. Nikolai Gregorievich was extremely fond of genuine Russian folksongs, and begged to hear some. The young people of the village did not need to be asked twice, and soon there was merry singing and dancing around us. This incident has always remained fresh in Peter Ilyich's memory, and fully nine years later a recollection made itself felt in the theme for the variations of his piano Trio, which is dedicated 'To the memory of a great artist,' that is to say, Nicholas Rubinstein. The music of *Snegourotchka* pleased Nikolai Gregorievich very much, and after the piece was struck off the repertory of the theatre, he performed it in its entirety, without the slightest abbreviation, at a concert, where it met with great success.

In 1886 Tchaikovsky wrote melodramatic music for one scene of Ostrovsky's tragedy *The Voyevoda,* which he had already treated as an opera, but this piece has remained in manuscript, and has probably little importance. Neither can his incidental music for *Hamlet,* composed in 1891, be considered as one of his prominent works. It consists of seventeen numbers, some of them quite fragmentary, scored for small

orchestra, the overture being a simplified version of the symphonic poem, with which we will be concerned presently.

There remain Tchaikovsky's ballets, three in number. They
all belong to the domain of fairyland, which is always a happy
background for a ballet. Before proceeding, it must be pointed
out that the ballet occupied a totally different position in Russia
from that which it held here. I have mentioned the three
companies at Moscow, occupying themselves respectively with
opera, ballet and the drama, but it should further be pointed
out that the standing popularly accorded them was about
equal. It was in no way considered more derogatory to the
dignity of a composer, as it then was in Western Europe, to
busy himself with the production of a good ballet than to
devote his energies to opera. The audience also was as keen
a judge of one as of the other, and the music of a Russian
ballet had to be of a quality which renders impossible any
comparison with the ballet music then tolerated in England.
The production of a new ballet in St. Petersburg was as
important an event as the production of a new opera. In
some cases it became a state function. It is therefore not surprising that many of the most eminent Russian composers from
Rubinstein to Stravinsky have contributed to this branch of
music.

Tchaikovsky's first ballet was *The Swan Lake,* which he was
invited to write by the directors of the Imperial Theatre at
Moscow. He began in August 1875 and sketched the first
two acts in a fortnight. The score was finished about the end
of the following March, and the ballet was produced at Moscow
on 4th March 1877. It was not then a success, though it
has become popular since. The reason for this is that it was
very poorly staged. The scenery and the costumes were
miserable, and the executants not much better. The ballet

master was utterly devoid of imagination and the orchestra was conducted by an amateur, who had never found himself face to face with so complicated a score. Consequently one can readily understand that the composer did not allow the failure to trouble him much. He remained perfectly cool during the month or so previous to the production, when, had it been an opera, he would have been in a state of high fever, and was perfectly indifferent to the result. The story told in the ballet is the following:

The young knight Siegfried has reached marriageable years but is still heart-whole. His mother wishes him to make his choice, and gives a great feast for this purpose. On the preceding evening Siegfried sees a flock of swans, and goes with his friends to hunt them, but the swans he has seen are the Princess Odetta and her attendant maidens, changed by magic and condemned by a demon to fly about in the daytime as swans, and resume their human form only at night. Siegfried sees Odetta and falls in love with her. She tells him of her pitiful fate, from which she can only be saved by the love and faithfulness of a pure heart. Siegfried declares he will be her knight. Odetta warns him that from the moment that he is unfaithful to her she will fall for all time into the power of the evil one. In order to prevent the betrothal of Odetta, the demon appears at the feast accompanied by his daughter Odelia, to whom he has given the form of Odetta. Siegfried chooses her for his bride, and is therefore unfaithful to Odetta, who must now be sacrificed to the demon. Odetta, however, escapes her fate by throwing herself into the water at night time, when she has human form. When Siegfried discovers his error and hears the news of Odetta's death, he also puts an end to his life, but the souls of both are reunited in the magic world of everlasting happiness.

The story is given here because it is typical of the fairy tales which the Russians love to see illustrated by a *ballet d'action*. In recent years it has become familiar in London through many performances. The music Tchaikovsky has written for it is graceful and attractive, but surpassed by that of his two later ballets. Certain numbers of it, for instance one of the waltzes, are amongst the things which every good Russian knows; but for the rest, the original score was frequently overladen. Tchaikovsky realized this in later years and gradually renovated the score by substituting new material, until the latest version—that which is used now—does not contain more than half of the original.

Tchaikovsky's next ballet dates from the summer of 1889 and is based on the well-known and well-worn fairy tale of Perrault entitled *The Sleeping Beauty*. This story is so dear to all those who have not forgotten the days of their youth, that the reader will not require a description of its incidents. The music is a great advance on that of *The Swan Lake*; in fact, as Rosa Newmarch puts it, it is, 'though not deeper than the subject demands, melodious in the best sense of the word, fantastic, brightly coloured; while it never descends to the commonplace level of the ordinary ballet music.' It consists of thirty numbers, many of which are gems of dance music. It was produced on 14th January 1890 at St. Petersburg. In 1921 Diaghilev presented it at the Alhambra Theatre in London in a sumptuous setting by Leon Bakst, with a cast including the greatest dancers of the day. But London, having meanwhile become accustomed to his 'triple bills,' did not give sufficient support, and the production, artistically a triumph, was a financial catastrophe. A portion of it has since been presented under the title *Aurora's Wedding*.

Its successor bears a title which is familiar to every English

Tchaikovsky lover: *Casse-Noisette* (*The Nutcracker*). It was begun in June 1891 and completed the following March. In view of the tremendous popularity of the music in this country, it is not entirely irrelevant to quote a few words from the composer's own pen. On 7th July 1891 he writes to Davidov as follows:

In accordance with my promise, I write to inform you that I finished the sketches of the ballet yesterday. You will remember that I bragged to you when you were here that I could finish the ballet in about five days. But I have scarcely finished it in a fortnight. No, the old man is breaking up. Not only does his hair drop out, or turn as white as snow, not only does he lose his teeth, which refuse their service, not only do his eyes weaken and tire easily, not only do his feet walk badly, or rather drag themselves along, but he loses bit by bit the capacity to do anything at all. The ballet is infinitely worse than *The Sleeping Beauty*—so much is certain; let's see how the opera (*Iolanthe*) will turn out. If I arrive at the conclusion that I can no longer furnish my musical table with anything but warmed-up fare, I will give up composing altogether.

How typical of the man is that quotation—rarely if ever believing in the excellence of his own work. In listening to the suite by which this music is best known in England, it is almost impossible to realize that Tchaikovsky could have written of it in such terms. Incidentally it may be mentioned that, when this suite was first performed at a symphony concert given by the Russian Music Society on 19th March 1892, five of the six numbers had to be repeated owing to the acclamations of the audience.

The subject is taken from Dumas's version of a fairy tale by E. T. A. Hoffmann. The scheme is as follows:

Act I. A Christmas tree in the house of President Silberhaus. The guests assemble and the candles are lighted.

Entrance of the children. After they have all received their presents, Councillor Drosselmeyer arrives with dolls which can move as if they were alive. To his favourite, Marie, the president's daughter, he gives also an ordinary old-fashioned German nutcracker in the shape of an old man who breaks the nuts in a capacious jaw; but this pleases the girl better than all her other presents. Her brother Fritz and the other boys snatch it away from her and break it. Marie bursts into tears, caresses the poor nutcracker and fusses about as if it were a real invalid, putting it to bed and rocking it to sleep. The party is over, all return home, and the candles of the tree are put out, but Marie cannot sleep and is still thinking of her nutcracker. At last she gets up from her little cot and slips down to have a look at it. It is midnight. Suddenly she hears mice approaching from all sides. Then a wonderful thing happens: the fir tree grows, and all the toys and the honey cakes come to life. Even the wounded nutcracker wakes up and moves. War is declared between the toys and the mice. Under the generalship of their king the mice easily defeat the honey-cake troops, but these are succoured in their extremity by the tin soldiers led by the nutcracker, and a heated battle takes place. The nutcracker fights with the king of the mice, and at the moment when the king seems to be getting the upper hand, Marie throws her shoe at him. He dies and the mice are defeated. The nutcracker, however, changes into a handsome prince, who thanks his saviour and takes her to his magic kingdom. They fly over the forest in winter, and each snowflake is to Marie a living thing.

Act II. The jam mountain, in the kingdom of sweets and titbits. The Sugarplum Fairy, who is queen here, awaits with her court the arrival of Marie with the nutcracker. When these arrive all acclaim the heroism of the little girl, and then begin the dances of the sweets.

The Sleeping Beauty and *The Nutcracker* were both arranged by the celebrated ballet master Marius Petipa, who was, in fact, responsible for all the best contemporary Russian ballets. It could not have been in safer hands, but the directions he found it necessary to give the composer must have proved somewhat irksome. Thanks to Modest Tchaikovsky's book, we are in a position to give a specimen of them.

No. 1. Musique douce. 64 mesures.

No. 2. L'arbre s'éclaire. Musique pétillante de 8 m.

No. 3. L'entrée des enfants. Musique bruyante et joyeuse de 24 m.

No. 4. Le moment d'étonnement et d'admiration. Un *tremolo* de quelques mesures.

No. 5. Marche de 64 mesures.

No. 6. Entrée des Incroyables. 16 m. rococo (*tempo* menuet).

No. 7. Galop.

No. 8. L'entrée de Drosselmeyer. Musique un peu effrayante et en même temps comique. Un mouvement large de 16 à 24 m.

La musique change peu à peu de caractère, 24 m. Elle devient moins triste, plus claire et enfin passe à la gaîté.

Musique assez grave de 8 m. et aussi temps d'arrêt.

La reprise des mêmes 8 m. et aussi temps d'arrêt.

4 mesures avec des accords d'étonnement.

No. 9. 8 m. d'un temps de mazourka. 8 autres m. de mazourka. Encore 16 m. de mazourka.

No. 10. Une valse piquée, saccadée et bien rythmée 48 m.

It speaks wonders for Tchaikovsky that, tied by such restrictions, he should have produced such excellent music. In spite of all his disparaging remarks, the *Casse-Noisette* is a charming creation. Its first production was not a remarkable success, partly owing to the illness of Petipa and partly to the fact that the audience did not reconcile itself readily to seeing children during the whole of the first act, where it was accustomed to seeing the usual ballet troupe. The part of the Sugarplum Fairy was entrusted to a lady who, although a highly accomplished artist, endowed with wonderful grace in her every movement, had the misfortune to be rather plain of feature, and possibly that was also resented. Be that as it may, the ballet has readily compensated for any lukewarmness in its original reception. For the guidance of those of my readers who may not know the place of the numbers of the suite, they had better be identified here. The miniature overture played entirely by the upper instruments of the orchestra, needs no description. The march which follows accompanies the entrance of the children in the first act. The dance of the Sugarplum Fairy is the last of all, just before the finale. The four dances which follow are taken from the divertissement of the sweets and toys in the second act. It is not indicated which of these is represented by the trepak, but the Arab dance stands for coffee and the Chinese for tea. The next number, entitled *Danse des Mirlitons,* is devoted to that delightful musical instrument of our youthful days, which consists of a piece of reed covered at each end with paper, producing a tone closely relating to that of a Jew's harp. The waltz is the movement immediately following the divertissement.

It is almost superfluous to point out to English readers how delightful these pieces are. To the genuine Tchaikovsky lover it is even a matter of regret that they should occupy the position they do in the public estimation, as their endless repetition, for instance at the 'Proms,' has been a bar to the production of many deserving works by the same composer which suffer comparative neglect. However, that is no occasion for the devotee to shed tears, for as long as the *Casse-Noisette* suite holds sway the fame of the composer will be kept green, and it is as well that he should be known by a piece in which he displays such extreme delicacy of touch, as the bulk of his orchestral work is of a nature to give one the impression that he was only at his ease when handling the heavier pieces of the musical armoury. Recently the ballet has been presented by the Vic.-Wells company.

CHAPTER IX

THE SYMPHONIES

WITH the *Casse-Noisette* ballet and the suite arranged from it for concert use we enter at last upon ground which is thoroughly familiar to English audiences. The introduction of Tchaikovsky's orchestral music into this country, so successfully accomplished by a few devoted pioneers, offers a convincing refutation of the charge so often raised against us that we are an unmusical nation. Our appreciation of Tchaikovsky has been at the same time prompter and warmer than that of any non-Russian country. For many years Germany eyed him with suspicion; his American tour was more or less a *succès d'estime*; to this very day he is unaccountably underrated in France. It is true that even here he acquired his popularity almost entirely with three works, of which only one belongs to his great and earnest achievements. The interest of the musical public has, however, been extended during recent years, and it is now no longer only the 'Pathetic' Symphony we hear, but also the fourth and fifth. It is curious that with all Sir Henry J. Wood's enterprise and his proselytism in favour of this composer, Queen's Hall should have been forestalled by a provincial undertaking in giving the complete series of the six symphonies. This honour is due to the late Sir Dan Godfrey, as conductor of the Bournemouth Symphony Orchestra. Recently Sir Thomas Beecham has given performances of the second and third Symphonies.

Tchaikovsky's magnificent record of symphonies must be dealt with first. These are divided from his programme music by a work which is at the same time a symphony and a tone-poem: *Manfred*. Using this imposing work as a bridge we pass to the series of symphonic poems, which is scarcely less important than that of the symphonies. Finally we have the four suites and various miscellaneous works to examine. Before proceeding, I shall venture to quote, to some extent as a motto for what is to follow, a passage from Edward Dannreuther's article on Tchaikovsky in the first edition of Grove's *Dictionary* :[1]

His compositions, more or less, bear the impress of the Slavonic temperament—fiery exaltation on a basis of languid melancholy. He is fond of huge and fantastic outlines, of bold modulations and strangely marked rhythms, of subtle melodic turns and exuberant figuration, and he delights in gorgeous effects of orchestration. His music everywhere makes the impression of genuine spontaneous originality.

Of all Tchaikovsky's works, not one, not even his operas, which he approached mostly with feelings of diffidence, caused him as much mental anxiety as his first Symphony, entitled *Winter Dreams*. It was the first work of any dimensions he engaged upon after emerging from his student's course at St. Petersburg. He commenced it at Moscow during the first year of his professorship (1866). We have already seen in the biographical chapters of this volume how he was assailed with nervous disorders of a pronounced kind, accompanied by frequent insomnia. We have also seen the disappointments and petty annoyances he was subjected to whilst endeavouring to secure a performance. It only remains to examine the music itself. Its title, *Winter Dreams*, suggests a poetic basis,

---

[1] The article in the later editions is by Rosa Newmarch.

which would give it the nature of programme music, but only two of the movements have any superscription indicating their descriptive meaning, these being headed *Dreams of a Winter Journey* and *Rugged Country—Cloudland*. The relation in which these poetic ideas stand to the music is that of providing the mood or *Stimmung*. They are not handled with any such approach to realism as one would expect to find if the work were a programme symphony. The music of the Symphony is interesting enough to have prompted any critic of well-developed receptivity at that period to prophesy great things for its author, but beyond that it has no great claim to immortality. The first movement is perhaps the most satisfactory. Possibly its pronounced melancholy threatens at moments to degenerate into mere sentimentality, but it is preserved by an underlying youthful ardour which does not fail to make itself felt whenever there is any such danger. Its weakness lies partly in its immature colouring, and partly in the unnecessary waywardness of its modulations. The *adagio* which follows contains some charming references to folksong, but the touch of the skilful hand is missed in their treatment, which suffers from lack of contrast. The scherzo, which was sketched at an earlier date than the rest of the work, might almost have been written by a predecessor of Tchaikovsky. It is an attractive and pleasing movement, full of musicianly qualities, but it is not Tchaikovsky. It contains not the slightest element of real modernity. It would almost seem as if the composer realized this himself, for he proceeds to assert his individuality in the finale with a boisterousness amounting almost to blatancy. In his later works his successful treatment of the brass is one of the most striking features. It is the one from which perhaps the most is to be learned, although his imitators seem hitherto to have profited by the lesson chiefly in a negative sense. In this finale it is evident that the craftsman has not yet attained that upper hand over his material which is the essence of artistic creation. His brass runs away with him. It is his master, and it prompts him to do things which no doubt he regretted in later years.

His next Symphony was composed between June and October 1872, and produced on 18th January 1873 at Moscow, under the conductorship of Nicholas Rubinstein. It is dedicated to the Moscow section of the Imperial Russian Music Society. Its success at the initial performance was so great that it was repeated 'by general request.'

Whilst he was writing it the composer declared his intention of endeavouring to pay greater attention to symmetrical form, in which, as he himself said, he had not hitherto greatly distinguished himself. Ultimately, he does not appear to have been very satisfied with the result, at least as regards the first two movements, but the finale was one of his favourite compositions.

Of the six Symphonies, this is the one which is the most subject to national influences. It was Kashkin who first gave it the name of the 'Little-Russian' symphony, which fits it well, most of the principal themes being of Malo-Russian origin.

The first movement is preceded by a comparatively lengthy introduction entirely derived from the following typical subject:

The manner in which this melody is handled is in itself sufficient to mark the great advance made by Tchaikovsky in the short interval which separates this from the first Symphony. The *allegro* itself belongs, as may be surmised from the foregoing, to the more orthodox of the composer's symphonic movements, but apart from the delightful *cantabile* which forms the contrasting second subject, it does not contain any features calling for special comment. It is succeeded by an *andantino marziale,* originally a part of the destroyed opera *Undine,* but the nature of which is, curiously enough, in close sympathy with the rest of the Symphony. Were its origin not known to us we should not have suspected that it was not part and parcel of the original scheme.

The scherzo is one of those rapid movements in 3–8 time, with which all of the Russian symphonists in turn have made us familiar. Its orchestration is scattered in a manner which enhances the humorous side of the composer's thoughts. As Knorr remarks, it is brimful of life and richly abounds in harmonic and rhythmical surprises. The trio, strangely naïve, is entirely derived from the following theme:

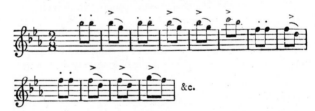

In the finale we are in the heart of the domain of folktune. The principal theme is a South Russian dance tune. It is a movement of almost overwhelming elemental strength, suggesting at moments a more primitive type of mankind. It is so convincing in its treatment, that even Cui, whose bitter antagonism to all Tchaikovsky's music is, as we have frequently seen, a blot on a distinguished career, refers to it frankly as 'magnificent' in his book on music in Russia. There is no doubt that it towers far above the rest of the Symphony, and ranks among Tchaikovsky's finest achievements. The principal subjects are given here:

The treatment given them is remarkable for two features: one is the use of the upper half of the hexatonic scale, introduced in the form of four descending notes in the extreme bass, thus:

Tchaikovsky

We have grown accustomed to this device, but although it was not an absolute innovation at this date, it was sufficiently

new to attract attention, and also some opposition. The other feature belongs to the latter development and consists of a long modulation built round sustained notes, as on page 110.

The orchestration is extremely brilliant, and the manner in which the interest is gradually worked up to a fine climax on the dominant pedal is masterly.

The third Symphony, in D major, was composed, according to a note on the manuscript, between 17th June and 13th August 1875, and it was performed for the first time at Moscow on 19th November of the same year. It consists of five movements—introduction and *allegro brillante, alla tedesca, andante,* scherzo, and finale *alla polacca.* The first time it was heard in England, at the Crystal Palace on 4th March 1899, it was announced as the 'Polish Symphony.' This title appears to have been suggested by Sir August Manns on account of the Polish rhythms occasionally used, and the composer did not raise any objection. The writer of the analytical notes, seizing upon this circumstance, invited the audience to weave quite a romantic programme round the Symphony, suggesting that it treated of 'Poland mourning in her oppression and rejoicing in her regeneration.' All this is the purest fantasy. There is in reality little that is Polish in the work. Berezovsky describes it as being distinguished from its two predecessors by the particularly western character of its music, which reflects partly the spirit of Schumann and partly the brilliance of the French school. Although cleverly constructed and attractively scored, this Symphony is not of overwhelming interest. It is as though Tchaikovsky were here using a language or idiom with which he is not entirely at ease. It does not strike one as the work of a Russian composer at all, and eclectic as Tchaikovsky undoubtedly was, he was not happy when the national element

III

was entirely relegated to the background. Both in contra-puntal resource and in instrumental colouring, however, considerable advance can be detected. The first three move-ments are the best and the finale the weakest. The scherzo is almost superfluous, its place being fully occupied by the waltz-like *alla tedesca,* but possibly the composer was not yet reconciled to the extreme step of substituting a waltz for the traditional scherzo, as he did in the fifth Symphony. The device he uses in the trio of this movement, of introducing the theme in seven different keys, over one sustained D on the horns, strikes one as being just a trifle too intentionally clever, and it is not wonderfully effective. On the whole, the waltz, which Knorr wittily describes as smuggled into this Symphony, is perhaps its most attractive feature.

Although a comparatively brief period separates the third and fourth Symphonies, this division represents the passing from the creation of merely good musicianly symphonies to that of works to which unquestionably the term 'great' must be applied. The fourth, fifth and sixth Symphonies belong to the giants of music. They look down from a pinnacle upon their predecessors, from amongst which only the finale of the second Symphony attempts to approach their level. The sketches of the fourth Symphony date from April 1877, and the composer, who was busy at that date with operatic work, nevertheless succeeded in finishing the orchestration before the end of the year. It is dedicated 'To my best Friend,' and it is not difficult to recognize the lady who is thus described as Nadezhda von Meck. Indeed, in his correspondence with her the composer refers to the work as 'your,' or 'our' Sym-phony. The original sketches bore the inscription that in case of his decease they were to be sent to her; and as the work progressed, and he gradually became inwardly convinced that he was surpassing all his previous attempts, his delight at the fact that he should do so in the very work he was writing for Mme von Meck knew no bounds.

The following letter, dated from Florence 1st March 1878 and addressed to Mme von Meck, is so vividly interesting that no apology need be made for quoting it in full:

How much happiness you letter has brought me to-day, dear Nadezhda Filaretovna! I am delighted beyond measure to learn that the Symphony has pleased you, that in hearing it you have also experienced the feelings which animated me during the task, and that you have opened your heart to my music. You ask if during the composition of this Symphony any definite programme was in my mind. To such a question I am accustomed to answer negatively. As a matter of fact, it is very difficult to give an answer. How can one describe those indefinite sentiments which fill one during the composition of an untitled instrumental work? It is a purely lyrical process. It is the musical confession of the soul, in which much material has accumulated, which now flows forth in tones, just as a lyrical poet expresses himself in verses. The difference lies only therein that music disposes of incomparably richer means, and is a more subtle language for the expression of the thousandfold different moments in the moods of the soul. Generally, the germ of the work appears with lightning suddenness, quite unexpectedly. If this germ falls on fertile soil—that is to say, when the desire to work is felt—it takes root with incredible strength and rapidity, shoots up from the ground, displays branches, twigs, leaves and finally blossoms. I cannot describe the process of creation otherwise than by this comparison. The greatest difficulty lies in the necessity that the germ should appear under favourable circumstances; then everything will proceed of its own accord. It would be vain for me to endeavour to express in words that immeasurable sense of happiness which comes over me when a new thought appears and begins to grow into definite form. I then forget everything and behave as if I were mad; all in me pulsates and vibrates; scarcely have I begun the sketches when thousands of details are chasing each other through my brain. In the midst of this magic process it sometimes happens that some shock from without tears me from my somnambulism—as, for instance, if someone suddenly rings, or if a servant enters the room, or if the clock strikes—and reminds me that it is time to leave off. . . . Such disturbances are absolutely terrible! Sometimes they frighten inspiration away for a time, and I must seek for it again—often in vain. In this case cold reason and technical resource have to be called in to assist. Often with the greatest masters there have been moments when the organic thread failed them and artistic crafts-manship took its place, so that parts of a whole appear to be glued together. But that is unavoidable. If that mood of an artist's soul which is called inspiration, and which I have tried to describe, were to last without interruption for any time, one could not survive it a single day. The strings would break and the instrument fall into a thousand pieces. It is already a good thing if the principal ideas and the general design of the composition are not arrived at by searching, but appear of their own accord under the influence of that supernatural, indescribable power which is called inspiration.

However, I have strayed from the point. For our Symphony there is a programme, or rather there is a possibility to describe its purport in words, and to you alone I will communicate the meaning of the whole work and of its separate sections. Naturally, I can only do it on broad, general lines.

The introduction is the germ of the entire Symphony.

That is fate, that tragic power which prevents the yearning for happiness from reaching its goal, which jealously strives that happiness and peace shall not obtain the mastery, that the heavens shall not be free from clouds—a power which constantly hangs over us like the sword of Damocles, and ceaselessly poisons the soul. This power is overwhelming and invincible. Nothing remains but to submit and lament in vain.

The feeling of depression and hopeless despair grows in strength and heat. Is it not better to turn away from reality and lull oneself in dreams?

Oh, joy! What a sweet vision has appeared! A radiant human being full of promise of bliss beckons to me.

How beautiful is hope! The insistent first motive of the *allegro* sounds now from a great distance. Little by little the soul is woven round with dreams. All that was dark, all that was joyless is now forgotten.

Joy! Joy!! Joy!!!

But no; these are but dreams; fate scatters them once more.

Thus our whole life alternates between grim reality and fluttering dreams of happiness. There is no safe haven. You are thrown hither and thither by the waves until the sea swallows you. That would be about the programme for the first movement.

The second movement shows suffering in another phase. It is that melancholy feeling which broods over us as we sit at home alone exhausted by work. The book which we have picked up to read slips from our hands, and a host of recollections arise. How sad that so many things have been and are past, but yet it is pleasant to think of one's youth. One regrets the past and has not the courage or the desire to begin a new life. One is somewhat tired of life, one would like to refresh oneself and look back, awakening many memories. One thinks of joyful hours, when the young blood still rushed and glowed, and there was satisfaction in love. One thinks also of sorrowful moments, of irreparable losses, but all that is so far, so far away. It is bitter, yet it is so sweet, to dive into the past.

In the third movement no definite feelings find expression. These are but capricious arabesques, elusive figures which flit past the imagination when one has drunk a little wine, and feels exuberant. The mood is neither sad nor merry. One thinks of nothing. One gives free reign to the imagination, and fantasy draws the most wonderful designs. Suddenly comes the memory of a tipsy peasant and a song of the gutter. . . . In the distance one hears military music passing. These are just the incoherent pictures which, as we fall asleep, suddenly float before our fancy and rapidly vanish. With reality they have nothing to do: they are incomprehensible, bizarre and disjointed.

Fourth movement. If you have no joy in yourself look around you. Go to the people. See how well they know how to be merry, and how heartily they yield to their happy feelings. The picture of a popular merry-making. Scarce have you forgotten your sorrow, scarce have you had time to become engrossed in the sight of the joys of others, when untiring fate once more announces its presence. The people do not trouble about you. They do not look at you;

they do not notice that you are alone and sorrowful. Oh! how happy they are! And you would affirm that all in the world is sombre and joyless! There is still happiness, simple, primitive happiness. Rejoice in the joy of others and—you can still live.

That is all I can tell you about the Symphony, my dear friend. Naturally, my words are not clear, nor are they exhaustive enough. Therein lies the peculiarity of instrumental music, that you cannot analyse its meanings.

It is getting late. About Florence I say nothing this time beyond that for my whole life I shall hold this town in pleasant memory.

PS. As I was putting the letter into the envelope, it occurred to me to read it again. I was alarmed at the imperfection and vagueness of the programme I have sketched. For the first time in my life the opportunity was given to me to put my musical ideas into words and phrases. I have only very badly solved the problem. Last winter I was continually depressed whilst working at this Symphony, and it is a real echo of my feelings. But still only an echo. Can it be forced into clear and definite sequences of words? I don't know, I don't understand it. Much I have already forgotten. There only remain to me general recollections of the sorrowful nature of my thoughts. I am very, very curious to see what my Moscow friends will say.

I spent last evening at the popular theatre and laughed very much. Italian humour is coarse, devoid of finesse and grace, but it carries everything with it.

Taneiev also asked Tchaikovsky whether this Symphony was to be considered as programme music or not, and in reply he was informed that certainly it had a poetic basis, which, however, could not be put into words. 'Moreover, I must confess to you that in my simplicity I had believed that the idea of this Symphony was so clear of comprehension that its general meaning could be grasped by all without a programme.' He vaguely described this meaning as being analogous to that expressed by Beethoven in his fifth Symphony, regarding which he did not admit the possibility of any difference of opinion as to the existence of a programme. 'If you have not understood it it is because I am no Beethoven.'

In his criticism of the first St. Petersburg performance Laroche spontaneously compared the wonderful opening with Beethoven's 'Thus Fate knocks at the door.' It is pleasant to note that on this occasion the critics were almost unanimous. Considering that with this Symphony the composer boldly proclaims his intentions of widening the symphonic form, and that innovation in this direction was apt to arouse antagonism on the part of the more conservative of his listeners, it is remarkable that it should have met with practically no opposition. Now, after the lapse of years, when its great beauties have obtained the fullest recognition, it might perhaps seem strange that these could have escaped any one at the time, but experience shows us that those compositions which proceed from the pioneers of music and are landmarks of progress rarely met with prompt appreciation, even though their lofty aim and artistic merits be obvious.

After the letter quoted above, there remains little to be said concerning the first movement. The beautiful melody which forms the principal subject of the *andante* is too lengthy for quotation, but one cannot forgo a mention of the delightfully delicate embroideries with which it is successively surrounded. Graceful as they sound, it will not escape the musician that they present from the technical point of view almost a model of counterpoint. The first part of the scherzo is played by the strings alone, *pizzicato* throughout. The composer appears to have had considerable misgivings as to the *tempo* at which this should be played. When first approaching Nicholas Rubinstein with a view to a performance of the Symphony, he intended to give him metronome marks for all its movements, but was deterred by the fact that, where he found himself, a metronome cost thirty francs. At that time he wrote that the quicker it was taken the better, but he admitted that he had no accurate conception of the speed at which it could be played *pizzicato.* A few weeks later he changed his mind and suggested to the conductor that it should not be taken so quickly; but he concludes by leaving it entirely to him, adding that he probably has a much better idea of the right *tempo* than the composer. The trio, a delightful piece of musical humour, is almost equally divided between the woodwind and the brass, each alone, the latter playing detached notes, which someone has described as a '*pizzicato* brass' effect!

In the gorgeous finale one point which, so far as I am aware, has escaped the compilers of programme notes, should be mentioned. The second subject is a Russian folksong, entitled 'In the fields there stood a birch tree,' which figures as No. 39 in Rimsky-Korsakov's interesting collection. The original rhythm of this song is triple, thus:

and Balakirev has used it in this sense in his *Overture on Russian Themes.* Tchaikovsky, however, adds two beats, making the rhythm quadruple, thus:

and the effect, if one is acquainted with the older version, is not altogether satisfactory. There is a characteristic vigour about the original, which is impaired by the redundant beats.

That may be a trifling blemish in a great work, and it is perhaps ungracious to mention it, but in the opinion of many the finale does not reach the level of the rest of the Symphony, and therefore one is to some extent justified in doing so.

Eleven years passed before the composer again wrote a symphony. The fifth, in E minor, was composed during 1888, and produced at St. Petersburg under the composer's directions on 17th November of that year. It was cordially received by the public, but the press was more doubtful this time, many of the critics being of the opinion that colour had claimed more of the composer's attention than actual musical thought. This is an instance of the very thing we were remarking in connection with the fourth. Considering that all over the musical world this Symphony is regarded as the equal and almost the superior of the famous 'Pathetic' Symphony, it seems incredible that its future was not foreseen. It has a musical motto:

which, after furnishing the introduction, recurs throughout its four movements, assuming in the finale its major form.

The frequency with which this Symphony is performed renders superfluous the actual thematic description, as in the case of its successor, the 'Pathetic,' for every concert-goer necessarily has a programme containing full analytical notes. Apart from its first movement, which is musically the most important, its two middle sections find the most favour. The slow movement is a perfect poem, and more than one writer has professed to find here the finest symphonic movement Tchaikovsky has bequeathed us. The waltz, which takes the place of the scherzo, is also a triumph, but rather of orchestration than of actual invention.

We have now reached Tchaikovsky's swan-song, the 'Pathetic' Symphony. This was written in the last year of his life, and writers have not been wanting who have read into the music a certain premonition of death. In justification of this a programme has been suggested which would make the basis of the work autobiographical. Indeed, the general opinion is that it is so, and it must be admitted that many details combine to strengthen the impression. There is, for example, in the first movement a passage, quoted in the earlier part of the present volume (page 6), which is taken from the Russian Requiem, and is construed as a reference to the early death of the composer's mother.

I am very reluctant to accept this hypothesis. Only one thing is certain, the existence of a programme, as in a letter to V. Davidov, to whom the Symphony is dedicated, the composer expressly mentions it, but refers to it as a puzzle for other people to break their heads over. It does not seem to fit in with Tchaikovsky's reserved and retiring nature that he should allow the circumstances of his own life to inspire a symphony. We are not dealing now with a work like Strauss's *Heldenleben*, which, however interesting, has very little real emotional appeal, but with a work which, with the single exception of its first performance, has everywhere obtained a hold on the most varied audiences. It is uncharitable to suppose that Tchaikovsky had no greater object than to make the world pity him or to indulge his own self-pity. Thus, regardless of what has been advanced in most other quarters and is almost universally accepted, we will dismiss the idea. Some years ago, not with the idea of seriously claiming that I had read the puzzle, but rather to prove that there was at least a possible alternative, I propounded a programme, the nature of which was mainly political, in the democratic sense. Reverence for the great departed prevented me from attempting any propaganda of this suggested programme, but it was with feelings of great sympathy that I perused the following lines in a then recent book by James Huneker:

Because of its opportunities for soul expansion, music has ever attracted the strong, free sons of earth. The most profound truths, the most blasphemous things, the most terrible ideas, may be incorporated within the walls of a symphony, and the police be none the wiser. Supposing that some Russian professional super-visor of artistic anarchy really knew what arrant doctrines Tchai-kovsky preached! It is its freedom from the meddlesome hand of the censor that makes of music a playground for great brave souls.

Beyond that let us be silent. The title of the Symphony was withdrawn by the composer himself before the first edition was printed, but it has obtained so firm a hold on the public that it would be inconvenient to discard it, although strictly speaking that would be the proper course. It was nevertheless irrelevant on the part of Hugo Riemann to attempt to account for this title by a superficial resemblance of the opening motive with that of Beethoven's 'Pathetic' Sonata.

We have seen that at the first performance the work fell flat, but this did not shake the composer's conviction that he had written the greatest of his works. On leaving the hall with Glazunov, to whom he also admitted the existence of a programme, he informed him that for the first time in his career he had come away from hearing one of his compositions with a feeling of complete content. His illness and death, which followed with such tragic suddenness, have been narrated elsewhere. In defence of the St. Petersburg public it must be remembered that at the second performance, which took place at the memorial concert, under Napravnik's conductorship, the listeners were carried away by their emotions to a degree which has seldom been witnessed at a symphony concert. It was as though the nature of the work then dawned upon them and literally appalled them.

For reasons which have already been stated, further description of so familiar a work will not be attempted here. Few readers can have missed hearing it; but to these, and also to those to whom it is well known, let one monition go forth: in spite of the proverbial tendency of familiarity, it should ever be approached with the utmost reverence.

Here terminates, properly speaking, our review of Tchaikovsky's symphonies, but there is one other work which logically belongs to it, although not bearing a number. This is the programme symphony of *Manfred,* which was composed during 1885 and produced on 25th March of the following year at Moscow. It is perhaps not a symphony in the strict classical sense, though it has as much claim to be considered so as, let us say, Berlioz's *Symphonie fantastique,* which it greatly resembles in construction. Berlioz's conception of a symphony with a poetic basis knit together by an *idée fixe,* musically identified with the central figure in the programme, has found much favour with Russian composers. Tchaikovsky's fourth and fifth Symphonies both owe much of their unity to the device, and as regards descriptive music there is a magnificent example by Rimsky-Korsakov, whose second Symphony, *Antar,* is constructed on the same lines. Tchaikovsky's *Manfred* belongs to the group of compositions which were inspired by the influence of Balakirev, and of which, as we shall see presently, his *Romeo and Juliet* is one of the most successful. Balakirev had been meditating on the subject of Manfred for some time, and had carefully elaborated a symphonic scheme, which, in the first place, he submitted to Berlioz during one of the latter's visits to Russia. The French composer, whether attracted by it or not, was unable to undertake it owing to his advancing years and indifferent health. Balakirev himself did not consider the subject a congenial one to his 'inner mood.' He therefore mentioned the matter to Tchaikovsky, whose *Francesca da Rimini* had so greatly impressed him that he considered him capable of doing it justice in the most brilliant manner. In his letter he says by way of preface, 'that the symphony, as with Berlioz, must have an *idée fixe*, the Manfred motive, which must go through all the movements.' Then he describes the four sections as follows:

I. Manfred wanders over the Alps. His life is ruined; many burning questions remain unanswered; nothing remains to him but memory. The form of the ideal Astarte floats before his fancy; in vain he calls to her; only the echoes of the rocks give back her name. His thoughts and memories burn his brain and eat out his heart; he seeks and pleads for oblivion which none can give him. (F sharp minor, second theme D major and F sharp minor.)

II. A mood entirely differing from the first movement. Programme: the customs of the Alpine huntsmen, patriarchal, simple and kindly. (*Adagio pastorale*, A major.) With these customs Manfred comes into contact, and is in sharp contrast. Naturally, you must first of all have a little hunting motive, only here the greatest caution is necessary so as not to fall into triviality. Heaven preserve you from commonplaces after the manner of German fanfares and hunting music!

III. *Scherzo fantastique.* (D major.) The spirit of the Alps appears to Manfred in the rainbow of the waterfall.

IV. Finale. (F sharp minor.) A wild *allegro* which depicts the caves of Arimanes, to which Manfred has gone in order to seek a meeting with Astarte. The contrast to this infernal orgy will be given by the appearance of Astarte's shade. (D flat major. The same motive as the D major of the first movement; there it was merely a reminiscence, which merged at once into the mature mood of Manfred; here, on the contrary, it can be brought to its fullest development.) The music must be light, clear, ideal and maidenly. Then a repetition of the pandemonium; then sunset and the death of Manfred.

Except that he reverses the order of the two middle sections, Tchaikovsky departs very little from this scheme. I quote here the Manfred motive, which permeates the work:

Beyond the above, which in its gloominess is a fine piece of characterization, I will not venture to quote musical examples for fear of being tempted too far afield.

As may be surmised, the first movement is not in the orthodox symphonic form, but the contrast between the two principal subjects, and the manner in which they are developed, goes far to justify the description of 'symphony' which follows the title of the work. The depicting of the various turbulent moods of the hero is accomplished in a most convincing fashion, and the opening towers in this respect far above the finale. The two middle sections belong really to the domain of musical landscape painting. The scene at the waterfall is irresistible. The Alpine episodes in the following section are slightly overburdened with imitative device, cleverly manipulated, but unimpressive; but the interest is quickened with the appearance of Manfred on the pastoral scene. The finale aims high and is gorgeous in the extreme. Unfortunately, its length makes it seem almost interminable, and its construction is not a little scrappy; but it has moments of absolute magnificence which make one forget its defects.

The *Manfred* symphony is not frequently performed. One reason for this is probably that it occupies an hour and five minutes. Another, and perhaps more forcible one, is that it is one of the most difficult orchestral works in existence. The difficulties are all legitimate. There is none of the acrobatic writing for unwieldy instruments which represents a later phase of modern orchestral scoring, but every lawful possibility of every instrument is taken the fullest advantage of, and the conductor's task is formidable. This means a vast amount of hard work for all concerned, and it is generally felt that, beautiful as the work undoubtedly is, it is not sufficiently great to justify the elaborate study required. Hence the few performances we have heard of this work are not likely to be the precursors of more numerous ones, but it is a matter for great regret that this should be so. *Manfred* is a work quite by itself, and therefore we are justified in giving it this special position between the symphonies and the symphonic poems.

Its relation to Schumann's great work is best described in the words of a German critic, who writes: 'While Schumann depicts the passion, Tchaikovsky reveals the agony of his hero.'

CHAPTER X

OTHER ORCHESTRAL WORKS

APART from *Manfred,* which I prefer to regard as a programme symphony and not a symphonic poem, Tchaikovsky's contributions to the latter form began with that entitled *Fatum.* He began to write it between 22nd September and 7th October 1868, and completed the sketch by 2nd November. The orchestration occupied him during November and December. It was played the first time by the Imperial Russian Music Society on 10th March 1869 under the conductorship of Nicholas Rubinstein. Almost immediately afterwards it was performed by the St. Petersburg branch of the Society under Balakirev, to whom it is dedicated. The work did not make a good impression in either centre. Although written without any more detailed programme than this title implies, Tchaikovsky allowed himself to be persuaded to preface it with some very inferior verses which his brother discovered for him. Both the critics and the public fell into the error of regarding the music as an illustration of this poem, which it was not intended to be. That is not, however, the only cause of the comparative failure of the work. It has grave defects, which were pointed out to the composer at the time by such friends as Laroche and Balakirev, and apparently Tchaikovsky himself gradually came round to their way of thinking, since some years later he destroyed the score. The

Paris 7 Mars 1888

Verehrter Herr Berger!
Ich komme in London
am 19ten an und werde
im Hotel Dieudonné, wie
Sie mir es geraten haben
absteigen.
Die Violinsolo partie (sie
ist im 1sten Geigen partie
gedruckt) schicke ich Ihnen
heute. Auf baldiges
Wiedersehen.
Ihr ergebener
P. Tschaïkovsky

FACSIMILE OF A LETTER TO FRANCESCO BERGER

parts still remained in the Conservatoire library, and from these the publisher M. P. Belaiev had the score reconstructed for publication in 1896.

From such unpromising beginnings Tchaikovsky moved with one step into the front rank of tone-poets with his Fantasy-Overture *Romeo and Juliet,* composed during September and November 1869, and produced on 16th March 1870, under the conductorship of Nicholas Rubinstein. In the following autumn it was entirely rewritten in the form in which it is now known to us. So much hangs on its dedication to Balakirev that some acquaintance with the circumstances becomes necessary before we proceed to consider the work. In consequence of the visit he paid to Tchaikovsky, Balakirev had become most enthusiastically interested in the young composer. One might almost say that the work was written under Balakirev's guidance. It was he who gave the first impetus. The very earliest sketches were sent to him for approval, numberless alterations were made in deference to his criticisms, and even the method by which Tchaikovsky courted the Muse was prescribed for him in a letter of 16th October, where Balakirev advises him to put on his rubber shoes, take a walking-stick and go for a walk on the boulevards, starting from Nikitsky.

'Let yourself become permeated with the subject,' he writes, 'and I am sure by the time you reach Sretensky you will have found some theme or episode.' He goes on to recommend him to meditate upon the first germ and carry it about in his head until something springs from it endowed with vitality.

It would take too long to go through the successive criticisms which every sketch submitted to him called forth, but which generally resulted in compliance with his wishes. Even when the work was complete he still had changes to suggest in it,

although he appears to have been pleased on the whole with
the result of his admonitions. The characterization of the music
is very good, in fact the entire work is based upon characterization rather than action.

A part from the opening theme which typifies Friar Laurence,
the work has two principal contrasted movements, the one
representing the feud of the Montagues and the Capulets, and
naturally all fire and animation, and the other the love-stricken
pair, all sweetness and romance. It closes in a manner
suggesting a reference to the final tragic scene. The strength
of the *allegro* is derived from its rhythmical features. Its
principal theme:

is already in this sense powerful, and it is worked up to a
climax of scale passages dominated by *fortissimo* chords in the
following startling metre, suggestive of clashing swords:

The principal theme of the love music is one of the most
beautiful Tchaikovsky has ever written:

It alternates with the following masterstroke:

The next work of this kind is the orchestral Fantasy (Op. 18) inspired by *The Tempest*. Although it has many fine moments, such as, for instance, the description of the sea and the storm, and the characterization of Caliban, it does not bear comparison with its predecessor. Above all, the love episodes do not receive nearly such inspired treatment as those in *Romeo*. As Knorr rightly observes, the love theme is most attractive when, entering *pianissimo,* it symbolizes the awakening of the tender passion, but when the splendour of the full orchestra shines upon it, it conveys an impression of triviality.

The next tone poem of this group, the Fantasy *Francesca da*

Rimini, is, in the opinion of most critics, the finest piece of programme music Tchaikovsky has produced. It surpasses the *Romeo* not only in maturity of conception, which under the circumstances is natural, but also in imagination. It was during his visit to Paris in 1876 that Tchaikovsky first began to plan a work on this subject. The preliminary sketches occupied him until October, but the orchestration, which is masterly throughout, even for such a master of tone colour, was completed in the incredibly short space of twenty-two days, and it was produced at a symphony concert at Moscow on 9th March the following year. It has three phases, of which the central one is by far the most important, as it depicts the narrative of Francesca, the beginning and end of the work providing the background of the Inferno. The agonizing picture brought to mind by the perusal of Dante is unmistakably portrayed in the opening and close of the work. The disconsolate wandering of the lost souls is represented by an *andante lugubre,* which merges into a veritable whirlwind, *allegro vivo.* The *andante* section is full of a haunting melody first played by the clarinet:

The subsequent accompanying figures, provided by three flutes, are among the most attractive features of the score. In the end the unhappy pair disappear once more into the whirling throng.

After Francesca, the next figure to attract Tchaikovsky was that of Hamlet, but it was not until twelve years later that he attempted to record his impressions in symphonic form. He wrote a Fantasy-Overture on this subject in 1888. Three years later he arranged an abbreviated and simplified version of it for small orchestra, together with incidental music in sixteen numbers to the tragedy. This later setting is naturally of much less importance than the original one with which we are now concerned. It is dedicated to Edvard Grieg, for whom Tchaikovsky had a warm admiration. As music, the work stands on the same high level as *Francesca*. It is beautiful throughout, but it does not possess the same appropriateness, and its illustration of the subject is not convincing. Whether it is that a Russian views Hamlet from an angle so different from ours that we cannot understand it, or whether the greater things of which Hamlet is a symbol have other meanings for Russians than for ourselves, Tchaikovsky's conception of the Danish prince is not one that comes readily home to the English Shakespearian. Still, against the music not a word can be said. The form it is couched in is far better thought out than is usually the case when so elusive a subject is chosen. Perhaps that also has something to do with the difficulty of reconciling it to the type of Hamlet. Liszt's poem with the same title, musically a far inferior work, is a closer realization of the character.

Only one more composition belongs to this group. It is the symphonic ballad entitled *The Voyevoda*. It was composed at Tiflis in the winter of 1890 and orchestrated the following year. Its poetic basis has no connection whatever with the composer's early opera of the same name, but is taken from some verses of Pushkin, which run somewhat as follows:

Late at night the Voyevoda comes back from the war. He orders silence, hurries towards the marriage bed, throws apart the curtains. . . . I was right! Gone! The bed is empty. Darker than the black night he lets fall his eyes full of ire; he pulls his grizzled moustache; then, tossing back his ample robe, he goes out and draws the bolt. 'Hola!' cries he, 'food fit for the devil! Why see I at the gate neither fastened bolts nor watch-dogs? Quick, my gun; get ready a bag, a rope, and take the carbine that hangs on the wall. Follow, I'll show my wife what vengeance can be!' The master and the young knave creep along the wall with stealthy eyes. In the garden, through the bushes, they see the white gown of the young wife. She is seated by the fountain, and a man lies at her feet. He is speaking. 'Nothing is left to me of our former happiness, of our early love. The sighs of thy soft bosom, the pressure of thy soft hand are sold to the Voyevoda. Years I sighed for thee, years I sought thee and thou wouldst not. The Voyevoda sought thee not; sigh for a woman he could not—the chink of his money brought thee to him. I have come through the dark night to see the eyes of my loved one, to press her soft hand. I have come to wish her in her new home prosperous years, much joy; then to fly from her sight for ever.' The fair one weeps and moans; the young man clasps her knees; the two behind the bushes watch. They rest their guns upon the ground, they pull cartridges from their belts, and, biting them, load with the ramrod. Stealthily they draw near. 'Master, I cannot aim,' whimpers the poor knave. 'Is it the wind? My eyes are moist; I shiver; my arm is weak; the fuse misses the pan.' 'Quiet, son of a dog, or I'll teach you to snivel. Prime again; aim—aim at her faithless forehead—to the left —higher—I'll undertake the gallant—be still—wait for the sound of my carbine—wait!' A gunshot rings through the garden. The young knave could not wait. A shriek from the Voyevoda— he totters.—The lad, it seems, aimed ill, the bullet pierced the Voyevoda's forehead.

It was performed at Moscow on 18th November 1891, at one of Siloti's concerts, and conducted by the composer. During the rehearsals Tchaikovsky already began to feel misgivings as to the success of the work, and by the time the performance was reached he had acquired almost a certitude that it was a failure, an opinion in which he was strengthened by some depreciating remarks by Taneiev. The performance was a bad one, chiefly owing to Tchaikovsky's own apathy, which communicated itself to the members of the orchestra. During the interval, in the artists' room, he destroyed the score, and ordered one of the attendants to bring him the band parts that he might do the same with them, but Siloti interfered; and endangered their friendship by informing the irate composer that in that building he, Siloti, was the host and Tchaikovsky the guest, and that his attendants would take their orders only from him. Thus the parts were rescued, and the score, subsequently reconstructed, was afterwards published by M. P. Belaiev. Tchaikovsky's dislike for the work was manifestly exaggerated. The poor reception it had was due to his conducting, as is proved by the success it has met with on its revival. Still, it has undeniable shortcomings, and even a tendency to slovenliness, although in one feature it ranks very high amongst the composer's works: that of rhythmical development. It is not the type of rhythmical waywardness which finds its expression in unusual time signatures, but a spasmodic disintegration of the melodies, whilst the metre is almost unaltered, producing an unsettled effect, and conveying readily the impression of an acute mental struggle. It is as if, tired of the dynamic means he so frequently used to achieve his end, he had aimed at something more subtle. For this reason alone we owe a debt of gratitude to Siloti.

Here terminates the list of Tchaikovsky's programme music, and our review of the works it comprises shows, above all, that Tchaikovsky interpreted his poetical subjects by a species of musical portraiture. Of action he reproduces little, of realism he attempts nothing, reserving his entire attention to the process of characterization. To say that he has always been successful would be indiscreet praise. Moreover, it is difficult to speak with certitude as, where we consider that he has failed to realize the poetic conception, he may have been thoroughly successful in representing his own idea of it. The means he uses, his alternation of elemental passion with pages of almost cloying sweetness, his gorgeous colouring and massive outlines, set their stamp on the music of his day. In their influence upon his successors it is probable that his symphonic poems have had more far-reaching effects than even the symphonies. Such a work as, for instance, *Francesca,* belongs to those which, as the French say, 'make school.'

Before taking our leave of Tchaikovsky's programme music it will be of interest to quote the composer's own view of that complex and controversial subject. It has been mentioned that the subject of *Manfred* was proposed to him by Balakirev. Nearly three years were to elapse before he acted upon the suggestion, the letter in question being dated 9th November 1882. On 24th November, presumably in reply, Tchaikovsky writes:

Notwithstanding my quite venerable age and considerable experience in writing, I must confess that up to now I am *wandering* in the boundless field of composition, vainly trying to find my true path. I feel that such a path exists, and I know that once I have found it I shall write something really good, but some fatal blindness constantly leads me astray and goodness knows whether I shall ever take the right road. Probably not. I think that first-class talents and geniuses differ from such unsuccessful people as myself in that they at once find their own broad road and pursue it, stepping boldly along and never looking back, to the end of their activity. Just now and again it has happened to me to get very near to my *path,* and then I have turned out things of which I shall not be ashamed to the end of my days, things which gladden me and strengthen my energy for work. But this has happened seldom and I certainly cannot reckon *Francesca* and *The Tempest* [works praised in Balakirev's letter] among these few exceptions. Both these things are written with merely affected warmth, with false pathos, with whipping-up of purely external effects, and are really extremely cold, false and weak. All this arises from the fact that these productions did not *arise out of* the given subject, but were only written apropos of it, i.e. the birth of the music was not inward but fortuitous, external. The meaningless uproar in the first part of *Francesca* does not correspond in the least to the stupendous grandeur of the picture of the infernal whirlwind, and the sham exquisiteness of the harmony in the middle part has nothing in common with the inspired simplicity and strength of Dante's text. Still less satisfactory and unworthy of its programme is that motley pot-pourri which bears the name of *The Tempest*. I say nothing of my *Romeo* overture which—God knows why—people have praised with as much exaggeration as they have belittled my other compositions. I remember that when I wrote it, being much affected by your sympathy and interest, I tried very hard to please you, but even then I was all too painfully conscious of the complete lack of connection between Shakespeare's portrayal of the youthful passion of the Italian Romeo and my own bitter-sweet moanings. I do not in the least think that programme music *à la Berlioz* is in general a false type of art. I am only pointing out the fact that I have done nothing of any significance in that line myself.

Undoubtedly this letter is coloured by Tchaikovsky's almost morbid self-depreciation, by the dissatisfaction with which, as a truly conscientious artist, he viewed his past achievements, conscious always of the desire to do better. But his reflections upon the nature of programme music are cogent, and his very pessimism affords a glimpse of the lofty ideal he kept before him, and, in his own view, never attained.

Tchaikovsky's overtures have much in common with his

programme music, inasmuch as, with the exception of the two unpublished ones in C minor and F major, referred to in the biographical portion of this volume, they are all three inscribed with titles which indicate their basis. The first of them is entitled *The Storm,* and was written for a drama by Ostrovsky. It is the one which he composed while still a pupil of the St. Petersburg Conservatoire, and we have already seen how it excited the ire of Anton Rubinstein. Viewed in the light of the course musical history has taken since that date, it is really not so alarming after all. Certainly it contains signs of premature emancipation, and some mild pulling of the check rein was called for, but there was no occasion for such violent anger as Rubinstein exhibited. The original plans for the overture display in an interesting manner the precocious gift of poetical construction which was such a valuable asset to the composer in later years. The scheme runs as follows: 'Introduction—*Adagio* (the childhood of Catherine and her life before her marriage). *Allegro* (reference to the storm—her longing for true love and happiness). *Allegro appassionato* (her mental struggle). Change of scene to evening on the banks of the Volga, again the struggle, but with traits of a certain feverish happiness. The forerunners of the storm (repetition of the theme which follows the *adagio* and further development of the same). The storm—the climax of the soul struggle and—death.' As the overture was published after the composer's death, the curious will be able to compare the form it ultimately took with this terse sketch of the first intention. The second Overture, that founded on the Danish national hymn, is, properly speaking, a *pièce d'occasion,* and the circumstances under which it was composed have already been described. Its construction is clear and unusually symmetrical, and although a work of comparatively minor calibre, Tchaikovsky himself, as we have already narrated, regarded it as one of his most satisfactory compositions.

The foregoing works, published and unpublished, belong to the composer's earliest period, all of them having been completed during the years 1864 to 1866. It was fourteen years before he returned to the true overture form, the works which he described as Fantasy-Overtures belonging entirely to the symphonic poem group. The overture entitled *The Year 1812* was commissioned for the All-Russian Exhibition of Arts and Crafts in Moscow, but actually performed at the consecration of the Cathedral of the Redeemer in the Kremlin on 20th August 1882. Besides the ecclesiastical ceremonies, there was to be a musical festival commemorating the events to which the building owed its origin, viz., those of 1812. It is said that the overture was to be performed in the square in front of the cathedral by an enormous orchestra, and that the bass drum part was to be entrusted to a company of artillery. It is not recorded whether the work was ever actually played under those conditions, but it is not improbable. Since the revolution the cathedral has been dynamited by the Bolshevists.

The material used consists of two well-defined original subjects interwoven with three others of historical import. The first of these:

from which the introduction is derived, and which recurs at

the end, is the Russian hymn, 'God preserve Thy people."
The second, the *Marseillaise,* does not need quoting. The
third is a folk-tune from the government of Novgorod, which
is also used in an *Overture on Russian Themes* by Rimsky-
Korsakov. The whole concludes with the Russian national
anthem. The sensational method of orchestration and the
importation of a peal of bells, suggestive of the Kremlin, has
earned for this overture a popularity which, in the composer's
own opinion and that of many of his admirers, it does not
deserve. True, it is a fine piece of musical construction, as
such, but there is a lack of subtlety about the whole conception
which jars on critical nerves. Even in the matter of appropriateness it is not beyond reproach, especially if one accepts the
statement that it purports to suggest the Battle of Borodino by
the musical conflict of the *Marseillaise* and the *Russian Hymn.*
As Rosa Newmarch points out, the latter was not composed
until 1833, and it is very doubtful whether the *Marseillaise*
was popular in the 'Grande Armée.'

With the last of the overtures, we leave the domain of programme music and return to the plane to which the symphonies
belong. Tchaikovsky's four suites present in some respects a
disappointing study. Leaving the fourth for a moment on
one side, as it is in reality an arrangement, the composer has
in each of the three remaining suites reached a great height in
certain pieces. Unfortunately, it is difficult to say of any one
of the three that it is in its complete form a great work. Before
I became acquainted with the circumstances of Tchaikovsky's
life, I was inclined to surmise that the juxtaposition of the
separate pieces which form these three works was sometimes
fortuitous, or even that they represented the periodical grouping
of movements which could not be utilized in any other way.
A little of this is borne out by fact. In each case the composer

FACSIMILE OF THE COMPOSER'S MANUSCRIPT

First Suite for Orchestra

was at first fascinated by some idea from which grew an orchestral piece, and subsequently he gave the resulting move-ment companions. In every other respect, however, this opinion was an injustice. In spite of the extreme looseness of their continuity, each of these three compositions was written with one impulse, and the imagined clearing out of the manuscript cupboard would have been so foreign to Tchai-kovsky's artistic nature that to have once harboured such a thought occasions some embarrassment.

The first Suite was written in 1878-9. Its germ was a scherzo which now figures as the fifth movement. From this starting-point the composer seems to have written a number of movements which he shuffled and reshuffled many times before the work reached its final form. The first sketch is described as consisting of: (1) *Introduction and Fugue*, (2) *Scherzo*, (3) *Andante*, (4) *Intermezzo* (*Écho du Bal*), (5) *Rondo*. This plan was, however, so much departed from that it is difficult to identify the various parts as subsequently modified. It is next described with the three last movements as: (3) *Intermezzo*, (4) *Marche militaire*, (5) *Dance of Giants*. It was already being printed in this form when the discovery was made that the entire suite was in duple time, and Tchaikovsky wrote in haste to Jurgenson begging him to cut out at least the march. For this he substituted a divertimento, approaching to waltz time, and the order of the pieces was once more changed. The march was retained, and the title of the last movement was, on account of its form, altered to *Gavotte*. Thus we reach the final disposition of the movements: (1) *Introduction and Fugue*, (2) *Divertimento*, (3) *Intermezzo*, (4) *Marche militaire*, (5) *Scherzo* and (6) *Gavotte*. In view of its extraordinary history, is it surprising that the work does not hang well together, and that the interest, which is at its highest point in the first movement,

141

has a tendency to flag before the end is reached? The work appears also to have given considerable trouble from the point of view of performance. After the first rehearsal, Serge Taneiev wrote to the then absent composer a long string of complaints which Rubinstein had made regarding the instrumentation, particularly in the woodwind. The composer's reply was emphatic and to the point, but concluded with a request not to communicate it to the eminent conductor, who, after all, contrived to secure a very successful performance. The *Introduction and Fugue* constitute one of the pearls of Tchaikovsky's orchestral repertory. The powerful subject of the fugue:

is of a nature well calculated to impress itself on the listener, and its assertiveness is enhanced by the masterly manner in which its several entries are scored, until towards the end, in its augmented form, it becomes almost overwhelming. Of the remaining movements the scherzo, which probably originated with greater spontaneity than the rest of the suite built round it, is the most pleasing and, incidentally, the most characteristic.

The second Suite was written in the autumn and winter of 1883. There are not so many details available as to how it originated, and although it was extremely well received on its first production, it was destined to be so completely overshadowed by the third Suite, which followed it at the interval of a few months, that it has ever since occupied a slightly subordinate position. It consists of: (1) *Jeu de sons,* (2) *Waltz,* (3) *Scherzo burlesque,* (4) *Rêves d'enfant* and (5) *Danse baroque* (*style Dargomizhsky*). The last is to some extent modelled on the *Casatchok,* a highly interesting but not a little grotesque composition by Dargomizhsky, founded on a Little Russian dance tune. It has, however, not quite the humour of its prototype.

The third Suite was begun on 28th April 1884 and finished on 4th June. Its development can best be described by a few excerpts from the composer's diary. At the first date mentioned he writes: 'Endeavoured, both at home and in the woods, to lay the foundation of a new symphony; remained discontented; took a walk in the garden, and found the germ of a future suite—not a symphony.' 29th April 1884: 'Wrote down a few thoughtlets.' 1st May: 'Angry about failure. Am very dissatisfied with myself because of the commonplace ness of everything that occurs to me. Am I really breaking up?' 8th May: 'In the morning I worked with all my strength at the scherzo. Wrote a little more after tea.' 12th May: 'Worked all day at the waltz for the Suite, but not with confidence of success.' 14th May: 'The waltz is giving me a lot of trouble. I must be getting old.' 20th May: 'Worked all the morning, not without trouble. However, the *andante* progresses.' (Later) 'I worked at and completed the *andante.* Am very pleased with it.' 23rd May: 'Have taken a dislike to the first movement of the Suite, after worrying the whole day over it. Decided to give it up and do something quite different. In the afternoon I rid myself of the un successful movement. What does it mean? How difficult I find it to work now! Can it be old age creeping on?'

24th May: 'After tea I once more attacked the horrible *Contrasts*, but suddenly a new idea struck me, and the thing began to flow.' 29th May: 'Played Mozart with great enjoyment. Idea for a suite from Mozart.' 30th May: 'I worked with as much ardour as if I were being driven. This strain is unhealthy and probably reflects itself in the poor Suite. Am working with much success. (The last variations before the finale.) Before supper, worked once more with energy, so as to be free to begin something to-morrow.' 2nd June: 'Have worked well to-day, and completed four variations. Took an early walk in the garden, and then worked until half-past twelve.' 4th June: 'The Suite is finished.'

The first performance of this Suite took place at a concert of the Russian Music Society at St. Petersburg, under the conductorship of Hans von Bülow, in the following January, and four days later it was played in Moscow under Erdmanns-doerffer. At both places the success was colossal, but the performance is reported to have been considerably better at St. Petersburg.

The work consists of four movements: (1) *Elegy*, (2) *Valse mélancolique*, (3) *Scherzo* and (4) *Theme and Variations*. The last-named section so entirely dominates its predecessors that it is enough to have merely enumerated them. The theme:

savours of folk music, except for the absence of the rhythmical waywardness which characterizes nearly all traditional Slavonic melodies. The variations stand in sheer plastic beauty above any modern set for orchestra, Elgar's *Enigma* Variations alone excepted. That is to say, that whilst it would be possible to enumerate a few other works in variation form which may surpass them in abstract musicianship, there is but one which combines this quality with the same degree of picturesqueness and power to please. It is the province of the analytical programme writer to describe the salient features of each variation, but it is no encroachment on that field to describe briefly the manner in which they follow one another. The first three are mainly contrapuntal elaborations, then follow, first a romantic setting in B minor forming a complete contrast, and next a vigorous *fugato*. The sixth variation is again melodic, but on leaving it we enter a series of what are, to all intents and purposes, Russian characteristic scenes. Consisting as they do of a chorale, a ballad-like declamatory song, a dance of the Little-Russian type and a mazurka in which the melody is entrusted to a solo violin, they represent well-varied phases, such as would easily furnish the basis of a set of independent pieces. Their logical conclusion is the polacca which forms the finale of the work. The use of the polonaise rhythm for all festive music on solemn occasions in Russia gives the selection of this rhythm for the last variation an appropriateness which might escape those who are not aware of the circumstance. It explains the extraordinary verve of the finish. It is preceded by a charming variation of the meditative order, which materially enhances its effect.

The fourth Suite, entitled *Mozartiana,* consists of orchestral versions of four movements of Mozart. The intense admiration Tchaikovsky had all his life for Mozart has frequently been referred to in the course of this volume. In 1887 occurred the hundredth anniversary of Mozart's opera *Don Giovanni,* and Tchaikovsky wished to commemorate the occasion by an act of musical homage. For this purpose he took the little *Gigue* in G major, a Minuet in D major, the Motet, 'Ave, verum corpus,' and the variations on a song from Gluck's comic opera *The Pilgrims to Mecca.* The orchestration is at the same time worthy of Tchaikovsky and free of any disrespect to the great classic. Naturally the work has met with considerable opposition from those musicians who consider any arrangement of this kind a piece of vandalism, but broaderminded critics will easily perceive that it is inspired by the most praiseworthy motives, and, as it stands, the Suite, although merely a *pièce d'occasion,* is a valuable if modest acquisition to the orchestral repertory.

The remainder of Tchaikovsky's orchestral compositions answer more or less to the same description. They consist of the *Capriccio italien,* a number of Marches written for various occasions and a Serenade for stringed orchestra.

The *Capriccio italien* is a bundle of Italian folk-tunes, partly, as the composer himself relates, taken from published collections and partly a record of the popular airs which caught his ear at Florence. It was begun at Rome in the early part of 1880, but not completed until after the composer's return to Russia. It is a piece of music which relies entirely on its orchestration for its effects; its musical value is comparatively slight, but the colouring is so vivid and so fascinating, and the movement throughout so animated, that one does not realize this when listening to the work. It is only afterwards that one experiences certain pangs of regret that such a rich garment should bedeck so thin a figure.

The Marches, although mostly symphonic, do not call for

much comment: as already stated, they were written for special purposes and almost to order. The first of them in order of date is at the same time the one which is most often played. It is termed *Marche slave,* and was composed in September 1877. It is constructed from a few South Slavonic or possibly Serbian airs, and the Russian national hymn. Its origin is due to a concert given for the benefit of the soldiers wounded in the war between Turkey and Serbia, which, at the time it was written, had already become merged into the Russo-Turkish War. Pan-Slavism was thus the order of the day and is writ large in the music.

Two years later, the same events caused Jurgenson to commission Tchaikovsky to write a Skobelev march in honour of the famous general, but the composer thought so little of it that for years it was allowed to sail under false colours, the composer's name being given as Sinopov. The *Coronation March* of 1883 was requisitioned by the town of Moscow. Beyond a general atmosphere of festivity it has no striking features. Neither the March composed for the law students in October 1885 nor the Military March written early in 1893 for the 98th regiment of infantry, which was commanded by the composer's cousin, Andrei Petrovich Tchaikovsky, are compositions of very serious importance.

Turning to Tchaikovsky's compositions for stringed orchestra, we are at once occupied with one of the most charming works he has bequeathed to the musical world, viz., the Serenade, Op. 48, which was composed some time in 1881 and performed for the first time at Moscow on 28th January 1882, when it had considerable success, both in the popular sense and amongst the professional section of the audience. Rarely, indeed, have such piquant effects been obtained without the use of the changes of colour rendered available by the presence of wind instruments in the orchestra. It consists of four sections. The first is a piece in the form of a sonatina, the two principal subjects of which, particularly the second, have an old-world air about them which takes one back to the days of the rococo. The waltz which follows is sprightly, and if its themes are a trifle exposed to the reproach of being commonplace, the dainty, somewhat Viennese treatment awarded them affords the fullest compensation. The third movement is an elegy that belongs to the composer's inspired moments. It strikes the one note of melancholy in an otherwise cheerful and even joyous work, but it is subdued melancholy, expressed in phrases of haunting beauty. The finale is derived from folk-tunes. Its introductory passage is based on a song which has its home on the towing-paths of the Volga near Nizhni-Novgorod (not the famous *Volga Boat Song*), but in its concluding bars the principal subject of the *allegro* is hinted at. This is a street song of the government of Moscow. Both are to be found in Balakirev's collection, where they figure as numbers six and twenty-nine respectively. The latter is quoted here:

It is an interesting example of the type of folksong the essence of which lies in its naïve repetitions. These afford the composer much opportunity for its introduction in varied forms, as, for instance, that of a persistent bass figure, on which

is built the climax preceding the recapitulation. This movement, although less weighty, deserves to rank with the finale of
the second Symphony, which it resembles in construction, as
a characteristic example of Tchaikovsky's treatment of national
music.

It seems as though it was the consciousness of having done
so well in the Elegy which figures in the Serenade, which
prompted Tchaikovsky to choose the same form in honour of
the memory of the actor Samarin, who died in 1884. This
piece even surpasses the earlier Elegy in beauty. It is but a
small, almost a fugitive, composition, and bears no opus
number, but its artistic qualities are very high.

CHAPTER XI

CHAMBER MUSIC

THE Serenade and Elegy for stringed orchestra, which are also capable of being performed as chamber music, afford us a good means of passing to the consideration of Tchaikovsky's contributions to this branch of music. Whether it be that smaller combinations possessed less attraction for him or that the high artistic plane attained in his orchestral works caused him to be so wedded to this form as to begrudge his efforts to any other, Tchaikovsky's achievements in chamber music are numerically out of all proportion to his orchestral works. Excluding an earlier Quartet, of which only one movement remains, and that in manuscript, his chamber music consists of three string Quartets, a string Sextet and the immortal Trio for violin, violoncello and piano.

In his valuable monograph on Tchaikovsky, Ivan Knorr, speaking of the quartets, points out recurring traces of what he happily refers to as homesickness for the orchestra. By this he does not mean that the composer, like many of his contemporaries and successors, has yielded to the temptation of writing what is really orchestral music for four stringed instruments. His genius, no less than his musicianship, was great enough to preserve him from that danger, but occasionally one feels that in the middle of his work a longing for more colour overcame him, and one can almost picture him pathetically wishing for possibly only a note or two from this or that wind instrument. His thematic development is, at least in the two later quartets, as masterly as one has reason to expect from a composer who was almost a wizard at the manipulation of a musical idea. His quartets will ever hold an honoured place among their kind, but it is doubtful whether even the most devout of his admirers will claim for him that he possessed the special genius for chamber music of a Mozart or a Beethoven.

The causes which led Tchaikovsky to the composition of his first Quartet, in D major, are pathetic. Want of money was not by any means an unusual circumstance in the earlier Moscow days, and in 1871 it had reached one of its especially uncomfortable phases. This led Nicholas Rubinstein to suggest to his young friend and colleague that he should give a concert of his own compositions; but neither the means at hand nor the prospects of the enterprise warranted the engagement of an orchestra, and as such a concert could not be given without at least one work of classic dimensions, Peter Ilyich decided to write a string quartet. This occupied him during the whole of February. Although not couched in his maturer style, the work is throughout characteristic of its author. None but Tchaikovsky could have written that opening movement, which is full of fresh and youthful fantasy. The following *andante cantabile* is derived from a folk-tune overheard at Kamenka. It enjoys the distinction of being one of the composer's greatest popular successes, and for this reason has appeared at various times in all possible arrangements, culminating in one for double bass with piano accompaniment. Though we may disapprove of this excess, we cannot but rejoice at the popularity which caused it, for the piece is no less a favourite with musicians than with the lay public. There occurs in the middle an attractive passage in which the melody is entrusted to the first violin, while the cello has a persistent figure of descending chromatic notes played *pizzicato,* the effect of which is both original and charming. It is interesting to note that after the composer's death, when more than one of his colleagues was honouring his memory in elegiac compositions, Arensky cleverly introduced into his a reminiscence of the beloved movement. The work in question, also a string Quartet, has for its middle section a set of variations on the theme of one of Tchaikovsky's songs, No. 5 of the set for children, Op. 54, and the manner in which this theme, inverted for the occasion, is coupled with the chromatic figure given here to the viola, brings to the mind a highly poetic picture, remotely related to the military custom of reversing arms at a funeral. The scherzo is slightly Schumannish, but in the finale the composer's individuality reasserts itself with confidence, the result being a movement of unmistakable vigour and even exuberance. On the whole, the work is one which owes the frequency with which it is performed rather to our affections than to our critical judgment. In spite of its admittedly great qualities, its conception remains somewhat primitive, when compared with those works on which the composer's fame is founded.

The second Quartet, in F major, was composed during the winter of 1873–4, and was first played privately at the house of Nicholas Rubinstein. It was then received with the utmost cordiality by every one present except the host's brother, Anton, who had nothing to say in its favour. On 22nd March following, its success was publicly established at a concert of the Imperial Music Society. This success was so marked, that the original edition was exhausted before the end of the season and a reprint became necessary; but it is significant that, on inquiry, only eleven copies were found to have been sold in Russia, the rest having been ordered from abroad. Tchaikovsky himself states that this Quartet was written practically at a stretch. That being so, it must have been during one of his periods of pessimism, for not a single ray of sunshine is allowed to show itself through the entire first movement. Great as is the advance in style from the Quartet in D to that in F, it must be admitted that this opening *allegro* is marred by occasional exaggerations of effect which are foreign to the spirit of chamber music. It is an impressive movement, with all its depressing influences, and perhaps it may be attributed to the convincing manner in which the pervading gloom is expressed that the scherzo which follows is invariably received with delight. This is couched on one of the irregular rhythms in the handling of which Tchaikovsky was such a consummate master. It really consists of seven beats, but these are barred as two measures of six-eight time followed by one of nine-eight, thus greatly facilitating the execution, which otherwise would present almost insurmountable difficulties of team-work. The *andante* is a fine piece of emotional music, although it suffers from a certain indefiniteness in the thematic material. As if to compensate for this, that of the finale is as concise as possible. This movement abounds in evidence of Tchaikovsky's contrapuntal facility. The simple themes are literally juggled with, with a fascinating dexterity, and the vivacity with which the interest becomes more and more excited is irresistible; indeed it largely contributes to ensuring the favourable reception which the Quartet as a whole invariably meets with.

Opinions differ largely as to whether this or the third Quartet, in E flat minor, can be described as the greater work. Sombre as they are, the ideas prevailing throughout the greater portion of the work just described seem more inspired than those of its successor, but in construction the third Quartet is superior.

It was written to commemorate the death of Ferdinand Laub, the eminent violinist, who had led the performance of both of Tchaikovsky's earlier Quartets, and it was first performed at a concert given by Hrimaly, who had also been associated with the production of its predecessors. It was sketched in Paris during 1876, and completed on the composer's return to Moscow. The elegiac suggestion underlying the work finds its principal expression in the slow movement, which is almost un-Christian in its pronounced fatalism, but the brightness of the scherzo which precedes it, and the verve of the finale, are well calculated to prevent the pessimism from becoming contagious. Musically this is the most important of the three Quartets. In it the composer comes nearest to realizing the atmosphere which appertains to this form. Even here he does not quite succeed in reaching the ideal, but in every other respect the artistic qualities are so great that he would indeed be a fastidious critic who would attempt to deny the work its place in the literature of the string quartet. Players of chamber music and their habitual audiences are dangerously inclined to regard the strict requirements of the form as something so utterly sacred and inviolable that unless they are complied with, sympathy is frequently denied. If Tchaikovsky has had less to suffer from this unreasoning attitude than many other modern composers, it is chiefly because his position as a musician was unassailable. Almost equally unassailable is the musical purport, in the abstract sense, of these two quartets, therefore it is incumbent upon us to lay stress on their intrinsic worth rather than the imperfections occasionally pointed out by the more austere votaries of chamber music, and which, after all, are somewhat problematic.

It was at a much later date that Tchaikovsky attempted once more a chamber work for strings alone, this time a Sextet. The title of the work, *Souvenir de Florence*, is a sufficient indication both of its purport and of its origin. It dates from his sojourn in Italy in the early part of 1890, was begun on 25th June, and completed in skeleton form on 12th July at Frolovskoye. It is dedicated to the St. Peters, burg Chamber Music Society, who gave its first public performance on 7th December 1892. It is a work of uneven merit. The ideas it contains are frequently a little common, place; but, as might be expected, this is atoned for by the treatment they receive. Particularly in the opening *allegro,* the finesse displayed is so fascinating as to cause one to forget for the moment how slender is the occasion for it. To do the composer justice, it must not be overlooked that he himself never regarded it as a serious work—indeed he frequently bestowed upon it the most opprobrious epithets. His severity was in this case excessive, as, with all its faults, it remains a pleasing and amiable composition, which one can always listen to with enjoyment, though perhaps the impression may not be a lasting one.

Only in one instance did Tchaikovsky bring the piano into his chamber music, but when he did so he out-distanced not only his own quartets but the great majority of the works existing in the form he adopted. The composition in question is the Trio for piano, violin and cello, in A minor, Op. 50, inscribed 'To the memory of a great artist.' This was Nicholas Rubinstein, who died in Paris on 23rd March 1881. It was natural that Tchaikovsky should wish to commemorate his close friendship with Nikolai Gregorievich, and it is consistent with the entire personality of Tchaikovsky that with such an incentive his inspiration rose to its highest level. The work is first mentioned about December 1881, and it was finished by the 25th January following, but it is probable that the sketches were commenced soon after the news of Rubinstein's death reached him. He exhibited the greatest solicitude as to the production of the work in a manner becoming to its object. Jurgenson was urged to make an *édition de luxe* of it, and Taneiev, whom every consideration designated as the pianist for the occasion, was given the most minute directions. In taking all this trouble the composer left his own claims out of the question. If he desired a sumptuous publication and a faultless performance it was solely that both should have the dignity due to their commemorative intentions. The work was performed at the Moscow Conservatoire on the first anniversary of Rubinstein's death, but it was not heard in public until 30th October following. On each occasion it was played by the three artists whom the composer from the beginning intended should be his executants, viz. Taneiev, Hrimaly and Fitzenhagen.

In spite of its length, the Trio consists of only two move-ments: (1) *Pezzo elegiaco* and (2) *Tema con variazioni*. The last of the variations, being developed at great length and ultimately merged into a tragic lament, is frequently looked upon as a separate movement, but logically it cannot be regarded as anything but a most fitting conclusion to the variations themselves and to the work as a whole. There is no attempt at sonata form. Were it necessary to analyse the first movement, the only standard by which one could do so would be that of a rondo. But what a rondo! Its dimensions and its depth so far outrun the usual aspect of this form that it is almost sacrilegious to give it that name. Let it be rather considered purely and simply as an elegy. From the first note to the last it compels one's sympathy. The accents of deep sincerity are absolutely convincing.

The variations are based on a theme to which I have already referred in connection with the picnic which took place after the performance of *Snegourotchka*. That was one of the best days the two friends had spent together, and among the memories of the departed which crowded round Tchaikovsky when thinking out this work, none fascinated him as this one. He gives the theme the freest possible treatment. Fantasy is allowed free rein, and instead of being treated with musicianly decorative patterns it is given the principal part in a series of beautifully contrasted pictures. Whether, as has been suggested, these pictures represent incidents of their friendship or salient points of Rubinstein's character and personality, is ground upon which it is indelicate to venture. To know that such was the case could not increase one's admiration for the work, but could only tempt one to a kind of posthumous eavesdropping. The melody takes the most varied forms, but possibly the most impressive is when it assumes the character of a plaint, which soars over arpeggio figures entrusted to the piano. Before that point is reached it has been heard as a dainty waltz and a vigorous fugue. Further on it appears as an animated and graceful mazurka, and so on in infinite variety until the powerful finale is reached, at the conclusion of which the principal motive of the elegy reappears stated in a most impressive manner. In Germany profound critics, taking themselves very seriously, have discovered in these variations a certain degree of gaudiness, and have not hesitated to allow that reproach to overshadow the work's great qualities. Such an opinion is not justified. True enough, the work does not keep to the dead level which is held in esteem by the musical authorities of the Fatherland, nor is it couched throughout in the chaste diction they prefer. Tchaikovsky had his own reasons for that. In the second place, even were there any justification for such criticism, it would still be artistically criminal to urge it in the presence of a work which compels admiration by its overpowering emotional message no less than the transparent sincerity of the sentiments it expresses.

CHAPTER XII

CONCERTOS

In proceeding with Tchaikovsky's remaining instrumental compositions we are obliged temporarily to revert to the orchestra, the first works calling for our attention being those for a solo instrument with orchestral accompaniment. These consist of three Concertos and a Fantasy for piano, a Concerto and two smaller pieces for violin, and a set of Variations and one smaller composition for cello.

Of all these works the best known is the famous piano Concerto No. 1, in B flat minor, Op. 23. This was written during November and December 1874, the orchestration being completed on 21st February 1875. The incidents which led to the suppression of the original dedication to Nicholas Rubinstein, and substitution of that to Hans von Bülow, are best described in a letter to Mme von Meck, dated 5th March 1878, in which the composer writes as follows:

In December 1874 I had written a piano Concerto! Not being a pianist, I considered it necessary to consult a virtuoso as to any points in my Concerto which might be technically impracticable, ungrateful or ineffective. I had need of a severe critic, but at the same time of one friendly disposed towards me. Without going into trivialities, I must admit that an inner voice protested against my selection of Rubinstein to judge the mechanical part of my work. However, he was not only the best pianist in Moscow, but undeniably a musician of great distinction, and I also felt sure that he would take offence if he should learn that I had passed him over and shown the Concerto to another pianist. Therefore I decided to ask him to hear the Concerto and make his observations concerning the solo part. On Christmas Eve 1874 we were invited to Albrecht's, and Nikolai Gregorievich proposed before going there that we should play the Concerto through in one of the classrooms of the Conservatoire. We did so. I brought my manuscript, and soon afterwards Nikolai Gregorievich and Hubert arrived. The latter is a very good and sensible man, but does not possess the smallest atom of independence. He is very talkative and diffuse, requires always a long preface before saying yes or no, is not capable of expressing his opinion in definite, unambiguous terms, and always ranges himself on the side of those who are strongest at the time. I must add, however, that this is done from lack, not of courage, but of character.

I played the first movement. Not a word, not an observation. If you only knew how uncomfortably foolish one feels when one places before a friend a dish one has prepared with one's own hands, and he eats thereof and—is silent. At least say something; if you like, find fault in a friendly way, but, for heaven's sake, speak—say something, no matter what! But Rubinstein said nothing; he was preparing his thunder, and Hubert was waiting to see what would happen, in order to join this or that side. As a matter of fact I did not require any opinion on the artistic form of my work; it was only the purely technical side which was in question. Rubinstein's eloquent silence had a portentous meaning. It said to me, as it were: 'My dear friend, how can I speak of details when the composition as a whole repels me?' I took patience and played the Concerto to the end. Again silence.

'Well?' said I, as I arose. Then sprang forth a vigorous stream of words from Rubinstein's mouth. At first he spoke quietly, but by degrees his passion rose, and finally he resembled Zeus hurling thunderbolts. It appeared that my Concerto was worthless and absolutely unplayable, that the passages were manufactured and withal so clumsy as to be beyond correction, that the composition itself was bad, trivial and commonplace, that I had stolen this point from somebody and that one from somebody else, that only two or three pages had any value, and all the rest should be either destroyed or entirely remodelled. 'For example, that! What is that, really?' (and then the offending passages would be caricatured at the piano), 'and that? How is it possible?' etc., etc. I cannot reproduce, what was worst, the accent and the voice with which Nikolai Gregorievich said all this. In short, an unbiased spectator of the scene could only have thought that I was a stupid, untalented and conceited spoiler of music-paper, who had had the impertinence to show his rubbish to a celebrated man. Hubert was astounded at my silence, and was probably greatly surprised that a man who had already written so many works and who taught composition at the Conservatoire could remain quiet and unprotesting under such a storm as one would not subject even a pupil to without examining his work with exhaustive care. Then Hubert began to add his comments to Rubinstein's, that is to say he agreed with him but attempted to put into milder words what Nikolai Gregorievich had expressed in such rough terms. I was not surprised at the whole affair, but I felt deeply offended. I had need of some friendly advice and criticism, which I shall probably always require, but here was no trace of friendliness. It was nothing but censure and depreciation, expressed in a manner calculated to wound me. I left the room without a word and went upstairs. I was so excited and angry that I could not speak. Soon afterwards Rubinstein came up to me, and seeing that I was very depressed, called me into another room. There he repeated that my Concerto was impossible and pointed to several places which required a thorough revision, adding that if these alterations were completed within a certain fixed time, he would play my Concerto in public. I replied that I would not alter a single note, and that I would have the Concerto printed exactly as it then stood. That is, in fact, what I have done.

This behaviour of Nicholas Rubinstein is the more difficult to understand because there can be no doubt that he really had a feeling of sincere friendship for Tchaikovsky. That he actually believed himself right in his judgment of this Concerto is indisputable, and he probably thought he was doing his young friend and colleague a service; but in the face of the greatness of the work itself that judgment is absolutely incomprehensible. It was nearly four years before Tchaikovsky could bring himself to forgive this incident, and then the first move came from Rubinstein, who, with that frankness and generosity which endeared him to his friends, spontaneously admitted that he had been absolutely at fault, that he had failed to realize the beauty of the work, and almost in so many words that he must have been unaccountably unintelligent on that occasion. Once that confession made, he threw himself heart and soul into the study of the Concerto and became one of its most frequent and most convincing exponents, both in Russia and elsewhere.

Tchaikovsky was not personally acquainted with Bülow, but he had heard through Klindworth that the famous pianist was an admirer of his works, which he had helped to introduce into Germany. Bülow was immensely flattered when Tchaikovsky announced his intention to dedicate the Concerto to him. Unlike Rubinstein, he raved about it, and professed to regard it as the most perfect of any works of Tchaikovsky's he was acquainted with. His letter of acknowledgment contains nothing but the warmest eulogy and concludes with hearty congratulations to all those who will enjoy the work in the future, whether as performers or as listeners.

The Concerto is in three movements. The first, *allegro non troppo,* opens with the following majestic theme:

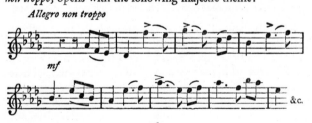

Allegro non troppo

mf

&c.

but its principal subject is in reality that introduced later:

which is taken from a folktune the composer heard once sung by blind beggars at a fair at Kamenka. Two other themes, which together form the second subject, deserve quotation on account of their characteristic beauty:

The middle movement embodies within itself the features of both the orthodox slow movement and the scherzo. The form is represented by an *andante semplice*, which furnishes the beginning and end of the movement, whilst its middle section is a delightful little dance piece somewhat savouring of a ballroom episode. Modest Tchaikovsky states that this movement contains an unconscious reminiscence of a French chansonnette which he and his brother Anatol heard sung by a popular vocalist, and which they were incessantly whistling about the house; but without more precise data we are unable to point out where this occurs. The finale is of the character of a Russian dance. It is full of vigour, and as great a strain on the muscular strength of the performer as the opening is on his technical proficiency.

As a whole the Concerto presents, from the musician's point of view, some defects of form, notably in the first movement, but from that of the pianist and of the listener it is irreproachable. It has become a supreme test of the interpretative powers of the socalled 'temperamental' pianist. The oldfashioned subdued and overscrupulous player cannot succeed with it. It requires a powerful grasp, both intellectual and emotional, and lies only within the province of the pianist who is fully alive to the fact that a concerto is not only a means for displaying either the composer's taste in embroidery or the pianist's command of technique.

The second piano Concerto, in G major, was written early in 1880, and played for the first time in public by Taneiev, 30th May 1882. It is not as grateful as its predecessor, which the composer never succeeded in equalling, nor was it favourably received. There can be no doubt that in proportion to the interest they are capable of arousing, the first two movements are too long. Then, again, the use of a solo violin and cello in the slow movement tends to relegate the piano so much into the background that it is not acceptable to the performer, nor entirely to the audience, which, after all, expects to hear a piano concerto. It is dedicated to Nicholas Rubinstein, a poor compensation for the loss of the honour Tchaikovsky intended to do him with the earlier work.

The third Concerto, in E flat major, places us somewhat in a difficulty. Strictly, there is no third concerto. In May 1892 the composer sketched a symphony, but he did not feel pleased with it, and although it was practically completed, it was, at least as far as the original symphony was concerned, destroyed. However, some of the material appears to have commended itself to him as the basis of a piano concerto, and the result was the one movement which figures in his opus list as Concerto No. 3, Op. 75. Although there is no reason why he should not have intended it to be a concerto in one movement, there is considerable evidence, both internal and external, that he did not. The internal evidence lies in the unsatisfactory impression it leaves. There is no sense of completeness about it. The external evidence consists of two other movements, *andante* and finale, which were found amongst Tchaikovsky's manuscripts at his death. They were originally conceived as the slow movement and finale of the discarded symphony, and the composer most probably intended to treat them as he had treated the first movement, but though completed they remained unorchestrated. They are preserved in this original version in the Tchaikovsky Museum at Klin. After the composer's death Taneiev scored these two movements for piano and orchestra and produced them on 20th February 1896. It is logical to assume that they complete the third Concerto, and yet somehow the separate parts do not seem to fit together as a whole. Naturally, one reason is the difference in the orchestration, although justice must be done to Taneiev, who did his utmost to adhere to the Tchaikovsky methods. But beyond that there is a dissimilarity of mood which baffles one.

In any case, the work or works will add little to the composer's glory. The infrequency with which they are played is alone almost sufficient to prove this, as it is well known that pianists would seize with avidity on another Tchaikovsky concerto if it presented possibilities of success. Good modern piano concertos are rare, as every pianist knows, and when one appears it does not have to wait many years for recognition.

The Concert Fantasy in two movements, Op. 56, dates from 1884, and was originally played by Taneiev at Moscow on 6th March 1885. Both there and later at St. Petersburg it had a great success, and there is much to show that this was due, at least as far as Moscow is concerned, to the popular personality of the performer. The work has not held its own in the repertories of the leading virtuosos. Nevertheless, it is effective and full of originality. It justifies its title by the poetic fantasy displayed throughout. The first movement is described as *quasi Rondo,* and is based on a theme which has a touch of folktune about it, without being absolutely of that type. The second movement, entitled *Contrasts,* was originally sketched as the first movement of the composer's third Suite, but whilst engaged on this work he took a temporary dislike to it and substituted the Elegy. When the suite was completed, this antipathy seems to have worn off, and the original idea was taken up again in concerto form. Its title is due to the utter divergence of two themes which, after being separately treated, are combined in a masterly manner.

The violin Concerto was begun in March 1878, at Clarens, and the sketches were completed by the end of that month, the orchestration occupying the composer until the end of April. It was originally dedicated to the distinguished Russian violinist Leopold Auer, but it did not at first appeal to him, and this, combined with its great technical difficulties, caused him to excuse himself from performing it. Nevertheless it was printed, but for two years no virtuoso appeared willing to grapple with the task. Then Brodsky played it at Vienna. Even he wrote to the composer that it was too crowded with difficulties, but he assured him that, these once overcome, its beauty was such as to tempt one to go on playing it for ever. This was Brodsky's first appearance at Vienna, and it was generally held that he was ill-advised to risk such a novelty under the circumstances. It was on this occasion that the critic Hanslick wrote in so bitter a tone that until his death Tchaikovsky could never forgive him; but he was not alone: all the leading critics of Vienna disapproved. The reason of this was that a large portion of the work is undeniably more pleasing to the performer than to the listener. The virtuoso, as he proceeds with the study of his part, becomes almost infatuated with it, but to the audience the excruciating difficulties, effective as they are, often convey the impression of an acrobatic performance. An exception must be made in favour of the delightful *Canzonetta* which forms the middle section of the Concerto. Originally the slow movement was a meditation, which the composer subsequently did not think worthy of its place, and which is known to violinists as No. 1 of the three pieces, *Souvenir d'un lieu cher,* Op. 42, the other two being a *Scherzo* and a *Mélodie.* As these three pieces are principally of drawing-room interest, and, moreover, the only original pieces for violin and piano Tchaikovsky ever published, this opportunity may be taken of including them in the present review, especially as they are occasionally performed with an orchestral accompaniment arranged by Glazunov.

The *Sérénade mélancolique* in B flat minor, Op. 26, for violin and orchestra, was composed in January 1875, and is dedicated to Leopold Auer. It is a singularly expressive little piece, depending entirely on melodic beauty for its effect. The *Valse-Scherzo*, Op. 34, is less interesting and descends at moments to the verge of triviality.

The one big work Tchaikovsky wrote for cello with orchestral accompaniment is the set of *Variations on a Rococo Theme*, Op. 33. The work was composed during December 1876 and dedicated to Fitzenhagen, whose name has been mentioned in connection with the piano Trio. It is known to all cellists as one of the finest display pieces in existence, but it has greater qualities than that. Each variation has a charm and piquancy of its own and is accompanied by orchestration of that lucid and dainty type of which Tchaikovsky was such a master when it suited his purpose. Not the least attractive feature of the work is the little *ritornello* which separates the variations.

The *Pezzo capriccioso* for cello and orchestra, Op. 62, was composed in 1889, and first performed by Brandukov, to whom it is dedicated. Although attractive to cellists, it is not a composition of the greatest importance.

CHAPTER XIII

PIANO MUSIC AND SONGS

THE number and importance of Tchaikovsky's piano works does not stand in the same proportion to his other compositions as is the case with most of the great masters. He was not himself a pianist of any remarkable attainments, and as a tone-painter he had an almost insatiable longing for the larger canvases. This is frequently visible in his efforts to produce greater variety of colour than the instrument is really capable of, the result being that most of his piano pieces seem to want orchestrating, and even those of which this cannot be said contain many passages the correct interpretation of which suggests stringed or wind instruments. It is not surprising that under these circumstances his method of writing was not always pianistic and that therefore his piano works have not received the same attention from virtuosos as his orchestral works from conductors. Modern writing for the piano is becoming more and more a specialized art, and, even in Russia, where versatility is more the rule than the exception, those composers who have reached the highest level of perfection in writing for the piano have mostly been men who have had difficulty in sustaining that level in other branches of music. Paradoxical though it may seem, whilst Tchaikovsky's piano compositions are pianistically open to adverse criticism, they nevertheless contain music which in the abstract is of the highest quality. Their list contains only two works in the larger forms, both piano sonatas.

The first of these, the posthumous Sonata in C sharp minor, was unearthed so late that it is not even included in the official thematic list of Tchaikovsky's published compositions. It contains some good material, amongst which must be mentioned that of the scherzo, subsequently utilized by the composer in his first Symphony. But this material is used in a weak manner, almost suggesting diluted music of the lesser German romantics, notably in the first and most important movement. As the work dates from Tchaikovsky's student days, it is perhaps not fair to criticize it, though, that being so, it was even less fair to publish it, after the composer had succeeded in concealing it during his lifetime.

The second Sonata, in G major, Op. 37, is quite another matter. It was composed during March and April 1878 at Clarens, is dedicated to Klindworth, and was played for the first time in public by Nicholas Rubinstein on 2nd November 1879, at Moscow. The reception given it was so cordial that the pianist repeated the work at his own recital. The interpretation was so magnificent that the composer considered the day one of the finest of his life. Nevertheless even the exponent's personality was not sufficient to cover up the defects of the work, which are those of most of the composer's piano compositions, to which may be added a lack of unity and occasionally a certain dryness. The most effective movement, from the point of view of the listener, is undoubtedly the finale. The first movement relies too much on musical dynamics to be a good opening for a piano sonata.

The remainder of the composer's piano works consists entirely of small pieces variously grouped. The first set is of two pieces, *Scherzo à la russe* and *Impromptu*. The former is contemporary with the posthumous Sonata, and dates therefore from his Conservatoire days. The theme it is based on is taken from a song which he heard the women sing when working in the garden at Kamenka. He first used it in the opening movement of his unpublished Quartet in B flat major. The piece was originally entitled *Capriccio*, and it chanced by accident that the manuscript book into which he wrote it also contained the *Impromptu*, which, however, was not intended for publication. Rubinstein gave the book as it stood to Jurgenson without informing him of this, and the latter published the pieces forthwith. At first the composer was inclined to be angry, but he soon reconciled himself to the accomplished fact.

The next set was the *Souvenir de Hapsal*, Op. 2, a reminiscence of the composer's escapade in Finland. The first and third pieces were actually written at Hapsal, but the second is a modification of a piece written at the Conservatoire. The third number, *Chant sans paroles*, has attained a world-wide popularity, which is attested by Jurgenson's having issued no fewer than seventeen different arrangements of it. In spite of its early date, it is one of the composer's most elegantly conceived small pieces.

This set was followed by the *Valse-Caprice*, Op. 4, and the famous *Romance* in F minor, Op. 5, both written in 1868. The latter belongs also to the representative pieces to be found in every Tchaikovsky album. It is a passionate song-like movement, interrupted by an *allegro*, the basis of which is a quaintly obstinate figure in the bass. The next pieces are a *Valse-Scherzo* in A major, Op. 7, and a *Capriccio* in G flat major, Op. 8, both composed in 1870. The former lacks distinction, but the latter is effective enough and deserves attention.

The following year saw the appearance of the three pieces, Op. 9, consisting of *Rêverie, Polka de salon* and *Mazurka de salon,* of which No. 2 is the most attractive. It was probably during his stay at Nice in 1871 that the two pieces, Op. 10, were composed. The first, a *Nocturne* in F major, is not well known, but its companion, the *Humoresque,* is extremely popular with pianists. Its middle section is a French folktune.

From this point the sets of pieces assume larger proportions. First we have the six pieces, Op. 19, composed at Moscow during 1873, and consisting of: (1) *Rêverie du Soir,* (2) *Scherzo humoristique,* (3) *Feuillet d'album,* (4) *Nocturne,* (5) *Capriccioso* and (6) *Thème original et Variations.* The most interesting number is the last, which is dedicated to Laroche. The theme is perhaps not stamped with marked individuality, and some of the variations are distinctly Schumannish, a fact of which the composer himself was conscious, as is proved by his indication over one of them. Nevertheless, the genuine Tchaikovsky finds room to assert himself, for instance in the *andante amoroso,* the chorale and the mazurka. The opening theme of No. 5 is quoted in the composer's diary, under date 11th June 1873, as the germ of a projected symphony. The material scarcely seems strong enough to have borne such a weight, and the composer was probably well advised in giving it its present form, but there are touches here and there which suggest a possible orchestral version. Of the remaining pieces, No. 3, principally on account of its brevity and facility of execution, has become a favourite with amateurs. Musically it stands far behind the scherzo, a thoroughly bright piece of piano writing, but making somewhat severe demands on the player.

The Variations just referred to are the only work in that form Tchaikovsky has bequeathed to pianists, but the writing of them seems to have suggested to the composer the possibility of a modification in the form itself, and thus we find his next work, Op. 21, consisting of six pieces on one theme. The composition is dedicated to Anton Rubinstein, but it seems to have taken the great pianist ten years to realize their worth. Then he repeatedly played them in public, but the composer in one of his letters remarks that, grateful as he was even then, it was not the same thing as if he had played them, or even any solitary piece of his, at that period. The pieces run as follows: (1) *Prelude,* (2) *Fugue,* (3) *Impromptu,* (4) *Funeral March,* (5) *Mazurka* and (6) *Scherzo;* and the modifications the theme encounters in becoming adapted to each successive form are chiefly of rhythmical character. This is one of the least known of Tchaikovsky's piano works, probably because it is the only one of them which does not belong to Jurgenson. It was given to the St. Petersburg publisher Bessel as a kind of incentive to hasten the latter's projected publication of the second Symphony, but Bessel in those days moved slowly, and it was a long time before the Symphony made its appearance. In recent years Wilhelm Backhaus has introduced the pieces at his recitals as a 'discovery.'

The next piano work was written to order. This is the set of twelve little pieces entitled *The Seasons.* The composer was commissioned by the editor of a certain St. Petersburg musical publication to write one piece per month, and Kashkin relates that he considered it a very easy and unimportant task. In order not to overlook it altogether, he instructed his servant to remind him on a certain date in each month that he had a piano piece to write, and in accordance with his orders, the servant came to his room on each occasion and remarked: 'Peter Ilyich, it is about time to send something off to St. Petersburg,' whereupon Tchaikovsky would sit down and write the piece straight off. Although of very modest dimensions, these pieces are for the most part delightfully lyrical in conception, and few of them, if any, bear any traces of the hurried way in which they were written. They were afterwards taken over by Jurgenson, and have since appeared in book form in many editions. The collection as a whole is immensely popular, but in this respect the *Barcarolle (June)* has deservedly outrun its companions. It is the most beautiful piece of a set containing many charming numbers.

The year 1878 saw the appearance of two well-known piano works, the twelve pieces of moderate difficulty, Op. 40, followed by the Album for Children, Op. 39. The twelve pieces were to some extent a selection from the composer's sketch-book. Thus the *Russian Dance* was originally intended for the ballet *The Swan Lake,* and the *Rêverie interrompue,* which closes the series, is a reminiscence of Venice, its middle section being a song the composer heard during his visit there. Probably the most generally known of the series is the *Chanson triste,* No. 2. Other attractive pieces are the *Chant sans paroles,* No. 6, the two Waltzes, Nos. 8 and 9, and the two Mazurkas, Nos. 4 and 5.

Barely were these pieces completed when the composer set to work on the Album for Children. This contains twenty-four little pieces of the most elementary kind, but not without interest even for advanced players. Many quaint ideas are used: for instance, the monotonous alternation of two chords, characteristic of that arch-enemy of Russian folk-music, the accordion, forms the basis of No. 12, whilst it is immediately followed by a paraphrase of the well-known *Kamarinskaya,* which has been so effectively orchestrated by Glinka. Some pieces have national colour. Among these may be cited an old French melody. Other numbers are purely lyrical, such as *Winter Morning* and *Song of the Lark.* The book concludes with a liturgical chant entitled *In Church.*

In 1882 Jurgenson, possibly thinking that the works he had published did not contain a large enough proportion of piano music, asked Tchaikovsky to write some more, and the result was six pieces, Op. 51, composed at Kamenka about the end of August 1882. The titles run thus: (1) *Valse de salon*, (2) *Polka peu dansante*, (3) *Menuetto scherzoso*, (4) *Natha-Valse*, (5) *Romance* and (6) *Valse sentimentale*. The best of the three waltzes is undoubtedly the first, which is a very attractive composition, but the most poetical number is the *Romance*, which is at the same time easy of execution. The polka is quaintly written, but contains some trivialities.

Tchaikovsky's next pianoforte piece, *Impromptu-Capriccio*, was a fugitive composition written for the Paris newspaper, *Le Gaulois*, which was issuing an album of music to its subscribers. Some time later it was reprinted in the Jurgenson edition. It consists mainly of a Russian dance motive, preceded and followed by a meditative *andante*. Much more ambitious is the piece entitled *Doumka* (*Scène rustique russe*), Op. 59, composed at the end of February 1886. It is dedicated to the head of the Paris Conservatoire, A. F. Marmontel. Like the majority of the composer's piano works, it undoubtedly suggests the orchestra. Its effects are massive and make some demands on the player, but its developments are almost entirely dynamic, and there is little real musical subtlety. From the pianist's point of view it is more a show piece than a source of pleasure. Two further isolated pieces were written during the year 1889, neither of them being regarded as of sufficient importance for the dignity of an opus number. The first is a *Valse-Scherzo*, in A major, which was not published until after the composer's death. The second is an *Impromptu* composed for an album dedicated to Anton Rubinstein, the pieces in which were contributed by former students of the

St. Petersburg Conservatoire. The impromptu consists merely of a pleasing piece of accompanied melody.

The next piano work to appear is, apart from the sonatas, Tchaikovsky's most important contribution to the literature of the instrument. It bears the date of the last year of the composer's life, but it is probably safe to assume that the eighteen pieces of which it consists represent the accumulation of occasional piano compositions written during the inter-vening years. These pieces are, for some reason or other, not as well known in England as the earlier set, which they, however, entirely surpass both in interest and importance. That is sufficient justification for the inclusion of a complete list of them: (1) *Impromptu*, (2) *Berceuse*, (3) *Tendres Reproches*, (4) *Danse caractéristique*, (5) *Méditation*, (6) *Mazurka pour danser*, (7) *Polacca de concert*, (8) *Dialogue*, (9) *Un poco di Schumann*, (10) *Scherzo-Fantaisie*, (11) *Valse-Bluette*, (12) *L'Espiègle*, (13) *Écho rustique*, (14) *Chant élégiaque*, (15) *Un poco di Chopin*, (16) *Valse à 5 temps*, (17) *Passé lointain*, (18) *Scène dansante : Invitation au Trépak*. Amongst these pieces there are none against which the reproach of triviality or commonplaceness can be levelled, even by the most fastidious, and many of them are gems. The *Berceuse* is an inspiration. It is an invidious task to select numbers for special mention, and the manner in which the ideas suggested by each of the titles is carried out is sufficiently successful to render such a course unnecessary. The majority of the pieces, except the one just mentioned, are difficult enough to demand a well-developed technique on the part of the performer, but in comparison with the composer's earlier pieces the difficulties they present are strictly pianistic and not due to his usual craving for colour. In short, these eighteen pieces are the most pianistic of all Tchaikovsky's compositions except, perhaps, the first Concerto.

Amongst the composer's papers at his death were found the sketches of an unfinished piano piece, which Taneiev carefully rescued and completed. It is the impromptu *Momento lirico*. This completes the list of Tchaikovsky's piano works.

Apart from his *Sixteen Songs for Children*, Op. 54, his songs amount to about eighty in all, grouped in various sets. The first six sets are of six numbers each. Of these thirty-six songs twenty-four are contained in an album published by Messrs. Novello & Co., with English texts by Lady Macfarren. The selection is a highly commendable one, containing all the popular favourites, such as 'None but a lonely heart,' the *Spanish Serenade* and the *Florentine Song*, 'If thou wilt hold my heart secure.' The next set was of seven songs, Op. 47, written in 1881, and contains at least one of great charm, No. 7, 'War ich nicht ein Halm auf frischem Wiesengrund.' Then follow the *Sixteen Songs for Children*, Op. 54. Unassuming as they are, they belong to Tchaikovsky's most charming creations. One of them in particular, that entitled *Legend*, has a melody of haunting sweetness. This is the theme referred to earlier as being that selected by Arensky for the variations in his second Quartet. The remaining sets consist of one of twelve songs, Op. 60, and three of six songs each, Opp. 63, 65 and 73. Tchaikovsky's genius as a song writer belongs to the borderland between the Teutonic and the Slavonic. His melodies are in most cases more emotional than a German song writer would have them, and their beauties of expression savour more of the physical than the intellectual. On the other hand, he was an accomplished lyricist, and though his methods may differ widely from those of a Schubert or a Brahms, he has bequeathed to us many songs of incontestable artistic greatness. It is particularly when dealing with a thought suggesting a certain languor that he is at his best.

His Slavonic temperament, without even then shaking off its eclectic trappings, makes itself convincingly felt.

Tchaikovsky's concerted vocal music is mostly religious, and as it is especially written for the services of the Orthodox Church, it possesses few features likely to be of interest to the reader. Of secular works in this category he wrote few. In the biographical section of this volume his examination Cantata, and also the coronation Cantata entitled *Moscow*, were referred to; but one other work deserves mention, viz., the Trio for two sopranos and contralto with piano accompaniment, entitled *Nature and Love*. This was written especially for the pupils of a teacher of singing, Mme Walzeck. It was produced at the composer's concert on 28th March 1871, but not published until after his death.

CHAPTER XIV

CONCLUSION

AFTER this survey of the compositions of Tchaikovsky, in the course of which generalizations in connection with each group of them have frequently arisen, there remains little to be said. His position in musical history is difficult to define. He certainly was one of the most inspired composers of the last century, reaching at moments a height of emotional appeal which could brook no denial. On the other hand it must be admitted that his works present great inequalities. It is not that he lacked self-criticism, nor the courage to denounce and even to destroy his own work when it did not please him, but this criticism, severe as it was, generally came after and not during composition. The result is that there are many works of his in circulation which he himself would have preferred to withdraw. A certain discretion is therefore required in dealing with them, and were it not that a volume like the present one must be nothing if not complete, it would have been preferable to confine attention to those works which impose by their greatness.

A word must be said here on the introduction of Tchaikovsky's orchestral music in England. When dealing with his Symphonies we noted that Sir Dan Godfrey, at Bournemouth, was the first conductor to give them seriatim, but with the exception of the first two, they were then no longer novelties.

The third, fourth and fifth Symphonies found their way to England in the first place through the Crystal Palace Concerts, the Richter Concerts and kindred undertakings. The famous 'Pathetic' Symphony would, had he lived, have been introduced under his own baton at the Philharmonic. His three visits, in 1888, 1889 and 1893, had been so successful that the Philharmonic Society obtained a half-promise from him that they should have the *primeur* of the symphony he was contemplating at the moment he left England. It was therefore appropriate that the society should have given the first performance of the Symphony, even though the regretted master had passed away, and this took place on 28th February 1894. The reception it met with caused it to be repeated on 14th March following, and almost immediately afterwards it appeared in the St. James's Hall programmes. It gained an instantaneous hold on the public. It is not too much to assert that not within a generation had a piece of pure orchestral music caused such a stir. Every one who could hold a pen wrote about it, and still the public could not learn enough. It flocked to each performance, and it is only in recent years that its interest has to any extent abated.

Of all our English exponents of Tchaikovsky, the first place belongs by right of conquest to Sir Henry Wood. Apart from the Symphonies, which he has given times without number, and, during one season, in their numerical order, this being the first London performance of at least two of them, he has conducted the first performances in England of a formidable list of Tchaikovsky's works, including such successes as the *Casse-Noisette* Suite. He introduced to English audiences that vivid programme symphony *Manfred*, the symphonic poems *The Tempest* and *Fatum*, the overtures to *The Storm* and *The Voyevoda*, the third Suite in its complete form (the variations having been performed separately on a previous occasion), the *Mozartiana* Suite, and many excerpts from his ballets and operas, the last being the symphonic tableau from *Mazeppa* entitled *The Battle of Poltava*. If Tchaikovsky's works are now so thoroughly familiar to English musicians, it is above all to Sir Henry Wood that it is due. It is astonishing that in the wear and tear of a Promenade Concert season the eminent conductor should have invariably had sufficient energy at his command to introduce a whole string of novelties into his programmes. Owing to the very nature of the circumstances, and the impossibility of obtaining adequate rehearsals from a band which had to perform every evening, some of the performances were not perfect, the chief flaw being a certain exaggeration of the heavier passages. To have avoided this entirely would have been miraculous, and on the other side of the account we have a long list of magnificent performances of the fourth, fifth and sixth Symphonies. In the 'Pathetic' Symphony especially Sir Henry has attained results which place him amongst the first conductors in Europe. In the others he has been surpassed, as for instance by Nikisch in the fifth, but in the 'Pathetic' he has held his own.

The genuine Tchaikovsky student has, however, one cause for complaint. The repeated performances of the 'Pathetic,' the *Casse-Noisette* Suite and the *1812* Overture were too persistent. True, Sir Henry found time to perform the other works, but generally speaking about once apiece. The result was that, whereas the 'man in the street' knew the *1812*, many well-informed concert-goers had the vaguest possible idea of such beautiful works as *Francesca da Rimini* or *Romeo and Juliet*. This state of things has since been remedied. We now hear the fourth and fifth Symphonies as frequently as the 'Pathetic.'

We repeatedly hear the variations from the third Suite and many other delightful works, though formerly a performance of them was an isolated function. But there is still room for a more general appreciation of Tchaikovsky's orchestral works. This must not be construed as a personal reproach to Sir Henry. He is a public man and he must respect the wishes of his public, which for many years would have its *1812* at any price, and if his programmes have since shown a wider choice it is chiefly because by his indomitable perseverance he has educated his public to the point of allowing him to do so—in itself a remarkable achievement.

Finally, on the assumption that a large preponderance of readers are probably pianists of greater or lesser attainments, it is felt that a few hints as to the piano arrangements by means of which Tchaikovsky's orchestral works can be approached at home would be acceptable. An arrangement for piano of a modern orchestral work is in the opinion of many musicians a somewhat mixed blessing. In the classical days such an arrangement had at least the merit of being a kind of photographic reproduction of the original, but with the expansion of the symphonic score, and the constant additions to orchestral effects, it can no longer claim to be that. It can, however, give one some more or less clear idea of the outline and the thematic construction of a work, and unless the composition is one depending primarily on its colour alone, the performing of a piano arrangement for self-instructive purposes at home is useful as long as one is careful not to treat it as an original piano work. It is after one has heard one or several orchestral performances of a work that the piano arrangement enters its proper sphere of usefulness—that of aiding the memory. Even the greatest orchestral work fades from the mind as the first impressions recede into the past, but occasional reference to an arrangement prompts the ear, which has an imagination and a memory of its own, to recall the orchestra, and therefore one's impressions retain much of their freshness.

All Tchaikovsky's orchestral works are arranged for piano duet. A few exist also for piano solo, but, generally speaking, they are almost unplayable in this form. For instance, to the ordinary pianist only one movement of the 'Pathetic' Symphony, the last, is accessible. The *Casse-Noisette* Suite is a fairly easy and effective solo, but in most arrangements the waltz is stripped of the varied counterpoints which are one of its principal charms in the orchestral version. The *1812* Overture has been well arranged by different musicians, but it is scarcely a work one would wish to play for one's own pleasure. Reverting to the arrangements for piano duet, the majority of them are well done and thoroughly playable. Certain isolated movements present great difficulty, such as, for instance, the waterfall scene in *Manfred,* and one work is almost entirely out of the question, viz., *Francesca da Rimini,* but otherwise the arrangements are within the reach of players of moderate proficiency, with the proviso that they must be good readers.

There is another form of arrangement which, in the case of modern works of great complexity, is far more useful than that of piano duets. This is a good setting for four hands on two pianos. The increase in effect is much greater than would be supposed. It is not only that the incessant crossing of parts becomes readily unravelled, but intelligent players, especially if they have some knowledge of the score, have an opportunity, by using a subtle variety of touch, of obtaining a certain limited amount of colour, thus imparting vitality to the rendering. There are also numerous arrangements for eight hands on two pianos, but these can safely be discarded as being inartistic. Perfect unanimity is not readily obtainable from four pianists, and it is extremely doubtful whether a performance of such an arrangement is ever really pleasant to listen to. For two pianos there exist arrangements of the two best movements of the second Symphony, of the entire 'Pathetic' Symphony, of the *Romeo and Juliet* Overture and the *Capriccio italien*. All these can be recommended with safety, although the nature of the last-named work scarcely warrants its inclusion with more interesting compositions.

Of the various selections from Tchaikovsky's operas, one only is well known: that on the themes from *Eugene Oniegin*, by Pabst, but that is a virtuoso piece of considerable difficulty.

This concludes our survey of the works of the great composer, and therefore brings the present volume to its close. The object has been throughout more to give the reader some modest assistance in attaining an accurate knowledge of the entire range of Tchaikovsky's compositions than to give a literary picture of the man, such as could at best be only incomplete, being derived from published records and not from personal experience. To those who desire such a picture there is one course open. The voluminous correspondence gathered from Tchaikovsky's papers by his brother, with the assistance of his friends in Russia, and systematically arranged in order of date, with interesting biographical matter where necessary, forms such a key to the composer's whole life, as well as his more intimate personality, as to leave little room for mystery. The Russian original has been admirably translated into German by the composer Paul Juon—assuredly a labour of love—and in our own tongue there exists, thanks to the indefatigable exertions of Rosa Newmarch, a version of most of the same material, but rearranged and re-edited with a view to making it more readable. Modest Tchaikovsky's book, with all its enormous value as a human document, is scarcely a literary production. Rosa Newmarch's is, and whereas in the former case the book might be laid down from sheer fatigue, in the latter one's attention is riveted to the end. Even had it been my intention to produce a work of this kind, it would have been quite impossible to do so within the dimensions of the present volume, and if the reader who has patiently travelled thus far arrives at the conclusion that he possesses something of the nature of a guide-book, the present task may perhaps be considered as successfully accomplished.

APPENDICES

APPENDIX A

CALENDAR

(Figures in brackets denote the age reached by the person mentioned during the year in question.)

Year	Age	Life	Contemporary Musicians
1840		Peter Ilyich Tchaikovsky born, May 7, at Kamsko-Votkinsk, son of Ilya Petrovitch Tchaikovsky, an inspector of mines.	Götz born, Dec. 7; Stainer born, June 6; Svendsen born, Sept. 30. Adam aged 37; Alabiev 53; Auber 58; Balakirev 4; Balfe 32; Berlioz 37; Bizet 2; Borodin 6; Brahms 7; Bruch 55; Bruckner 16; Cherubini 80; Chopin 30; Cui 5; Dargomizhsky 27; Delibes 4; Donizetti 43; Franck 18; Gade 23; Glinka 37; Goldmark 10; Gounod 22; Halévy 41; Heller 25; Henselt 26; Lalo 17; Liszt 29; Lvov 41; Mendelssohn 31; Mercadante 45; Meyerbeer 49; Moniuszko 20; Mussorgsky 1; Offenbach 21; Ponchielli 6; Reinecke 69;

Year	Age	Life	Contemporary Musicians
			Rossini 48; Rubinstein (A.) 10; Saint-Saëns 5; Schumann 30; Serov 20; Smetana 16; Spohr 56; Spontini 66; Strauss (J. II) 15; Varlamov 39; Verdi 27; Verstovsky 41; Wagner 27.
1841	1		Chabrier born, Jan. 18; Dvořák born, Sept. 8; Pedrell born, Feb. 19.
1842	2		Boito born, Feb. 24; Cherubini (82) dies, March 15; Massenet born, May 12; Sullivan born, May 13.
1843	3		Grieg born, June 15; Sgambati born, May 28.
1844	4	Takes piano lessons from Fanny Durbach, the governess of his elder brother Nicholas and his cousin Lydia, whom he soon overtakes.	Rimsky-Korsakov born, March 18.
1845	5	A music mistress, Marie Markovna Paltchikov, is engaged, under whom he makes rapid progress at the piano.	Fauré born, May 13.
1846	6	Plays the piano unusually well for his age.	
1847	7		Mackenzie born, Aug. 22; Mendelssohn (38) dies, Nov. 4.

Year	Age	Life	Contemporary Musicians
1848	8	Removal to Moscow, where T.'s father is disappointed in his prospects of a new appointment, Oct. Removal to St. Petersburg, where T. is sent to a boarding-school and has music lessons from Philipov.	Donizetti (51) dies, April 8; Duparc born, Jan. 21; Parry born, Feb. 27; Varlamov (47) dies, Oct.
1849	9	Severe nervous trouble brought about by overwork at school and abnormal sensitiveness. Removal to Alapaiev, where T.'s father has secured an appointment as works manager on the Yakovlev mines.	Chopin (39) dies, Oct. 17.
1850	10	Makes progress in music and begins to compose. Sent to the School of Jurisprudence in St. Petersburg, Aug.	
1851	11	Preparatory studies at the School of Jurisprudence. T. lives with various friends of the family, who are still at Alapaiev.	d'Indy born, March 27; Lortzing (48) dies, Jan. 21; Spontini (77) dies, Jan. 14.
1852	12	Return of the family to St. Petersburg.	Alabiev (65) dies; Stanford born, Sept. 30.
1853	13	Studies at the School of Jurisprudence continued.	
1854	14	T.'s mother dies of cholera, June.	Humperdinck born, Sept. 1; Janáček born, July 4.

Year	Age	Life	Contemporary Musicians
1855	15	⎫	Chausson born, Jan. 21; Liadov born, May 11.
1856	16		Kastalsky, born, Nov. 28; Martucci born, Jan. 1; Schumann (46) dies, July 29; Sinding born, Jan. 11; Taneiev born, Nov. 25.
		Studies at the School of Jurisprudence continued.	
1857	17		Elgar born, June 2; Glinka (54) dies, Feb. 15.
1858	18		Leoncavallo born, March 2; Puccini born, June 22; Smyth (Ethel) born, April 23.
		⎭	
1859	19	Leaves the School of Jurisprudence and enters the Ministry of Justice as first-class clerk.	Ippolitov-Ivanov born, Nov. 19; Liapunov born, Nov. 30; Sokolov born, March 26; Spohr (75) dies, Oct. 22.
1860	20	Works at the Ministry of Justice and dabbles in music without showing very exceptional promise.	Albeniz born, May 29; Charpentier born, June 25; Mahler born, July 7; Wolf born, March 13.
1861	21	Visit to London, Paris, Germany and Belgium as companion and interpreter to a friend of his father's, July–Sept. Although still holding his post at the Ministry of Justice, he begins to study harmony under Zaremba (40), but he is not yet sure that a	Arensky born, Aug. 11; Catoire born, April 27; MacDowell born, Dec. 18; Marschner (66) dies, Dec. 14.

Year	Age	Life	Contemporary Musicians
		musician's career is open to him.	
1862	22	Still continues his studies with Zaremba (41) as an amateur. His failure to secure a vacant post at the Ministry of Justice induces him to devote himself professionally to music. He enters the newly opened Conservatoire, but still retains his official post.	Debussy born, Aug. 22; Delius born, Jan. 29; Halévy (63) dies, March 17; Verstovsky (63) dies, Nov. 17.
1863	23	Resigns his post at the Ministry of Justice, spring. He finds himself in straitened circumstances and earns but little by giving lessons. He continues to study theory under Zaremba (42) and goes to Rubinstein (33) for orchestration.	Mascagni born, Dec. 7.
1864	24	Studies at the Conservatoire continued. Overture to Ostrovsky's (41) drama, *The Storm* (Op. 76), composed, summer.	Grechaninov born, Oct. 25; Meyerbeer (73) dies, May 2; Strauss (R.), born June 11.
1865	25	Summer holiday with his sister, Alexandra Davidov, at Kamenka. On his return to St. Petersburg a hard struggle begins. Nicholas Rubinstein (30) engages T. as professor of	Dukas born, Oct. 1; Glazunov born, Aug. 10; Sibelius born, Dec. 8.

Year	Age	Life	Contemporary Musicians
		harmony at the newly opened Conservatoire of Moscow.	
1866	26	Arrival in Moscow, Jan. Composition of Symphony No. 1, G minor (Op. 13) gives him infinite trouble and leads to a nervous disorder, April. He spends a holiday at Miatlev with his sister's mother-in-law, Mme Davidov, and her daughters, Elizabeth and Vera.	Busoni born, April 1; Kalinnikov born, Jan. 13; Rebikov born, June 1.
1867	27	Opera, *The Voyevoda*, to a libretto by Ostrovsky (44), begun, spring. Visit to Finland. Summer holiday with the Davidovs at Hapsal. 3 piano pieces, *Souvenir de Hapsal* (Op. 2), dedicated to Vera Davidov. Return to Moscow, Aug. Meeting with Berlioz (64), who conducts two concerts there, Dec.	Granados born, July 29.
1868	28	Visit to St. Petersburg, where he meets Balakirev (32), Cui (33), Dargomizhsky (55), Rimsky-Korsakov (24) and Stassov (44), Easter. Visit to Berlin and Paris, summer.	Bantock born, Aug. 7; Rossini (76) dies, Nov. 13.

Year	Age	*Life*	*Contemporary Musicians*
		The Voyevoda put into rehearsal at Moscow. Friendship and growing intimacy with Désirée Artôt (33), his engagement to whom he announces to his father, Dec. Symphonic Poem, Fatum, finished.	
1869	29	Artôt (34) marries Mariano Padilla (27) at Warsaw, without an explanation to T., Jan. Production of The Voyevoda, Feb. 11. Opera, Undine, begun, Jan., and finished, July. After a summer holiday at Kamenka he returns to Moscow, where he meets Balakirev (33) and Borodin (25). Fantasy-Overture, Romeo and Juliet, suggested by Balakirev, begun.	Berlioz (66) dies, March 8; Dargomizhsky (56) dies, Jan. 17; Pfitzner born, May 5; Roussel born, April 5.
1870	30	Chorus for an opera, Mandragora, composed, but the work abandoned, Jan. Opera, The Oprichnik, begun, Feb. Romeo and Juliet produced, March 16. Visit to St. Petersburg, where Undine is rejected, May. T. is summoned to Paris to see	Balfe (62) dies, Oct. 20; Koreshchenko born, Dec. 18; Lvov (71) dies, Dec. 16; Mercadante (75) dies, Dec. 17; Novák born, Dec. 5; Schmitt (Florent) born, Sept. 28.

Tchaikovsky

his pupil and friend Vladimir Shilovsky, who is consumptive. They go to Soden and attend the Beethoven Festival at Mannheim. T. visits Nicholas Rubinstein (35) at Wiesbaden. Departure for Switzerland on the outbreak of the Franco-Prussian War, July. After a stay at Interlaken, T. visits Munich and Vienna on his way back to Russia. Return to Moscow, end of Aug. *Romeo and Juliet* revised, Oct.

1871   31   String Quartet No. 1, D major (Op. 11), composed, Feb. Meeting with Turgenev (53), who attends the first performance of the Quartet, March 28. Summer holidays spent at Kamenka, Nizy and Ussovo, with his sister, Alexandra Davidov, and his friends Kondratiev and Shilovsky respectively.   Auber (89) dies, May 12; Serov (51) dies, Feb. 1.

1872   32   Opera, *The Oprichnik,* finished, May. Festival Cantata for the opening of the exhibition celebrating the 200th anniver-   Juon born, March 9; Scriabin born, Jan. 6; Vassilenko born, March 30; Vaughan Williams born, Oct. 12.

Year	Age	Life	Contemporary Musicians
		sary of the birth of Peter the Great, June 12. Symphony No. 2, C minor (Op. 17), begun at Kamenka, June, and finished at Ussovo, Aug. Scoring of the Symphony completed, Oct.	
1873	33	Second Symphony produced by the Moscow Musical Society, Jan. 18. Music to Ostrovsky's (50) fairy-tale, *Snegourotchka*, begun, April. Visit to Germany, Switzerland and Italy, June–Aug. Overture to Shakespeare's *Tempest* (Op. 18) begun at Ussovo, Aug. It is first performed in Moscow, Dec.	Rachmaninov born, April 1; Reger born, March 19; Tcherepnin (N.) born, May 15.
1874	34	String Quartet No. 2, F major (Op. 22), composed, Jan. *The Oprichnik* produced at St. Petersburg, April 24. Visit to Italy, spring. Opera, *Vakula the Smith*, begun during a holiday at Nizy and finished at Ussovo, end of Aug. Piano Concerto No. 1, B flat minor (Op. 23), composed. It is intended for Nicholas	Holst born, Sept. 21; Schoenberg born, Sept. 13; Suk born, Jan. 4.

Year	Age	Life	Contemporary Musicians
		Rubinstein (39), but being severely criticized by him, it is dedicated to Hans von Bülow (44), Dec.	
1875	35	Suffers from great depression and finds his teaching at the Conservatoire very irksome. Symphony No. 3, D major (Op. 29), begun at Ussovo, finished Aug. Ballet, *The Swan Lake* (Op. 20), commissioned by the Moscow Opera. Production of the third Symphony in Moscow, Nov. 19. Taneiev (19) plays the first Moscow performance of the piano Concerto, Dec. 3. Meeting with Saint-Saëns (40), who visits Moscow, Nov. T. visits Paris with his brother Modest (25), Dec.	Bizet (37) dies, June 13; Glière born, Jan. 11; Ravel born, March 7.
1876	36	String Quartet No. 3, E flat minor (Op. 30), begun, Feb. Visit to Vichy, where he has been ordered the waters, July. He goes on to Bayreuth, where he meets Liszt (65) and calls on Wagner (63), who fails to receive him. He hears the *Ring* with admira-	Akimenko born, Feb. 20; Falla born, Nov. 23; Götz (36) dies, Dec. 3.

Year	Age	Life	Contemporary Musicians

tion and dislike, Aug. After a visit to his sister Alexandra Davidov at Verbovka, he returns to Moscow in great depression. He decides that he should marry. Symphonic Fantasy, *Francesca da Rimini* (Op. 32) finished, Oct. The opera, *Vakula the Smith,* produced at St. Petersburg, Dec. 6. Meeting and friendship with Tolstoy (48) and beginning of correspondence with Nadezhda von Meck (44), who much admires T's work and is anxious to relieve him of all pecuniary embarrassments, Dec. *Variations on a Rococo Theme* for cello and orchestra (Op. 33), Dec.

1877 37 Ballet, *The Swan Lake,* produced in Moscow, March 4. First performance of *Francesca da Rimini* at a Moscow symphony concert, March 9. T. again suffers from mental depression, spring. Symphony No. 4, F. minor (Op. 36), begun, April.

Dohnányi born, July 27

Year	*Age*	*Life*	*Contemporary Musicians*
		T. works at an opera on Puskhin's poem, *Eugene Oniegin*. Marriage to Antonina Ivanova Milyukov, July 18. Driven to despair by an irresistible aversion to his wife, he leaves alone for Kamenka, Aug. 7. Return to his wife in Moscow, Sept. He suddenly leaves for St. Petersburg in a state of mind bordering on madness, Oct. 6, and is ordered a complete change by the doctor. A final separation from his wife is inevitable and he leaves for Switzerland with his brother Anatol (27), settling at Clarens, Oct. Nadezhda von Meck (45) offers him an annuity of 6,000 roubles. Visits to Italy and Vienna. T. remains in Venice.	
1878	38	Removal to San Remo, Jan., and to Florence, Feb. Fourth Symphony and the opera *Eugene Oniegin* finished, Jan. Return to Clarens, where the violin Concerto (Op. 35) and	

Year	Age	Life	Contemporary Musicians

Life

the piano Sonata (Op. 37)
are begun, March. The
Sonata and 12 piano
pieces, *The Seasons* (Op.
37A), finished at Kamenka,
April. Holiday spent at
Brailov, the estate of
Nadezhda von Meck (46),
who is absent, May. Re-
turn to Moscow, Sept. He
finds his duties at the Conservatoire quite unbearable
and resigns his professorship, in which he is suc-
ceeded by Taneiev (22).
Composition of Suite No.
1 for orchestra (Op. 43) at
Kamenka and departure
for Florence, Nov.

1897 39 At Clarens again, where
the opera *Joan of Arc*, based
on Schiller's *Maid of Orleans*, is begun, Jan. Visit
to Paris, Feb., where the
work is completed, March
6. Return to Russia for
the production of *Eugene
Oniegin* in Moscow, March
29. Summer holidays
again spent at Kamenka
and Brailov. When
Nadezhda von Meck (47)
returns home, Aug., T.
moves on to her smaller

Contemporary Musicians

Bridge (Frank) born, Feb.
26; Ireland born, Aug.
13; Respighi born, July 9;
Scott (Cyril) born, Sept.
27.

Year	Age	Life	Contemporary Musicians

estate of Simaki. They have never met. Piano Concerto No. 2, G major (Op. 44), finished at Kamenka, Oct. Departure for Rome, Nov.

1880 40 — *Capriccio italien* for orchestra (Op. 45) begun in Rome. Death of father, Jan. 24. Return to Russia, March. The *Capriccio* finished at Kamenka, spring. Visits to Brailov and Simaki, summer. Serenade for strings (Op. 48) and Overture, *1812* (Op. 49), finished at Kamenka, Oct. The latter was commissioned by Nicholas Rubinstein (45) for the Moscow Exhibition. — Bloch born, July 24; Krein (G.), born, Jan. 16; Medtner born, Jan. 5; Offenbach (61) dies, Oct. 4; Pizzetti born, Sept. 20; Wieniawski (45) dies, March 31.

1881 41 — Production of *Joan of Arc* at the Maryinsky Theatre, St. Petersburg, Feb. 25. After a visit to Italy and France the directorship of the Moscow Conservatoire, vacated by the death of Nicholas Rubinstein, is offered to T., who declines it, April. At Kamenka that summer he makes a study of Russian church — Bartók born, March 25; Miaskovsky born, April 20; Mussorgsky (42) dies, March 28; Rubinstein (N.) (46) dies, March 23; Vieuxtemps (61) dies, June 6.

Year	Age	Life	Contemporary Musicians
		music, edits the works of Bortniansky and writes a first Vesper Service (Op. 52). Visit to Rome, Nov. Meeting with Liszt (70) at a concert organized in his honour, and with Sgambati (38), who plays there, Dec. 6.	
1882	42	Serenade for strings (Op. 48) produced at Moscow, Jan. 28. Piano Trio (Op. 50), dedicated to the memory of Nicholas Rubinstein, finished, Jan. 25. Return to Russia, April. First performance, at the Moscow Art and Industrial Exhibition, of the second piano Concerto, with Taneiev (26) as soloist, May 30 and the *1812* Overture, Aug. 20, at the consecration of the Cathedral of the Redeemer in the Kremlin.	Kodály born, Dec. 16; Malipiero born, March 18; Raff (60) dies, June 25; Stravinsky born, June 17.
1883	43	Visits to Berlin and Paris, Jan. – May. Opera, *Mazeppa*, based on Pushkin's poem, *Poltava*, finished, summer. Suite No. 2 for orchestra (Op. 53) finished at Kamenka.	Bax born, Nov. 6; Casella born, July 25; Flotow (71) dies, Jan. 24; Gniessin born, Feb. 4; Krein (A.) born, Oct. 20; Szymanowski born, Sept. 21; Wagner (70) dies, Feb. 13.
1884	44	Productions of *Mazeppa* in	Smetana (60) dies, May 12.

Year	Age	Life	Contemporary Musicians
		Moscow, Feb. 15, and St. Petersburg, Feb. 19. Suite No. 3 for orchestra (Op. 55) finished, May. Command performance of *Eugene Oniegin* at the Imperial Opera in St. Petersburg.	
1885	45	Is elected director of the Moscow branch of the Russian Musical Society and moves to a country house at Maidanovo near Klin, Feb. Composition of the symphonic poem, *Manfred* (Op. 58), undertaken on Balakirev's (49) advice, finished, and that of the opera, *The Sorceress*, begun, Sept.	Berg born, Feb. 7.
1886	46	First performance of *Manfred* in Moscow, March 25. Visit to Tiflis, where the Musical Society gives a concert and dinner in his honour, April. Departure for Paris by sea. May and June spent there. He meets Delibes (50), Fauré (41), Lalo (63), Ambroise Thomas (75) and Pauline Viardot-Garcia (65). Return to Maidanovo, end of June.	Liszt (75) dies, July 31; Ponchielli (52) dies, Jan. 17.

Year	Age	Life	Contemporary Musicians
1887	47	First performance of *Chere-vichki* (*The Little Shoes*), also called *Oxana's Caprices,* a new version of *Vakula the Smith,* Jan. 31. T. makes his first appearance as concert conductor, at St. Petersburg, with a programme of his own works, March 17. Visit to his brother Anatol (37) in the Caucasus. From there he is called to Aachen to see his friend Kondratiev, who is critically ill, July. Suite, *Mozartiana* (Op. 61), finished there, Aug. 10. Production of *The Sorceress* at the Maryinsky Theatre in St. Petersburg, Nov. 1.	Borodin (53) dies, Feb. 16|28.
1888	48	Begins his first international tour as conductor at Leipzig, where he sees Désirée Artôt (53) again and meets Brahms (55), Busoni (22), Delius (25), Grieg (44), Reinecke (64) and Ethel Smyth (30). He conducts the Gewandhaus Orchestra, Jan. 5, and the Liszt - Verein gives a Tchaikovsky Festival, Jan.	Alexandrov born, May 13|25.

Year	*Age*	*Life*	*Contemporary Musicians*
		6. Concerts conducted at Hamburg, Jan. 19, and Berlin, Feb. 8. Visit to Prague, where he gives two concerts and meets Dvořák (47), Feb. Arrival in Paris, Feb. 24. Two concerts given there. Meeting with Gounod (70), Massenet (46) and Paderewski (28). One of the London Philharmonic Society's concerts conducted in London, March. After his return to Russia, T. takes possession of a country house at Frolovskoye, April. Symphony No. 5, E minor (Op. 64), finished, Aug. First performances, in St. Petersburg, of the fifth Symphony, Nov. 17, and of the Fantasy-Overture, *Hamlet* (Op. 67), Nov. 24. Visit to Prague to conduct *Eugene Oniegin*, Nov.	
1889	49	Second international concert tour. T. conducts at Cologne, Frankfort, Dresden, Geneva and Hamburg, Feb.–March. Visit to Paris and London,	Henselt (75) dies, Oct. 10.

Year	Age	Life	Contemporary Musicians
		conducting the Philharmonic Society's concert there, April. Ballet, *The Sleeping Beauty* (Op. 66), finished at Frolovskoye, summer. T. conducts a festival in honour of Rubinstein (59), for which he has composed the *Homage to Anton Rubinstein* for male choir and an *Impromptu* for piano, Nov.	
1890	50	Production of *The Sleeping Beauty* in St. Petersburg, Jan. 14. Opera, *The Queen of Spades*, to a libretto by his brother Modest (40), based on Pushkin, composed in Florence, Jan. – March. String Sextet, *Souvenir de Florence* (Op. 70), composed at Frolovskoye, June. *The Queen of Spades* produced in St. Petersburg, Dec. 19. Rupture with Nadezhda von Meck (58), whom he has never met face to face, Dec.	Feinberg born, May 26; Franck (68) dies, Nov. 8; Gade (73) dies, Dec. 21.
1891	51	Performance of Shakespeare's *Hamlet* with incidental music (Op. 67A) by T., Feb. 21. St. Petersburg Opera com-	Bliss born, Aug. 2; Delibes (55) dies, Jan. 16; Prokofiev born, April 23.

Year	Age	Life	Contemporary Musicians
		missions a one-act opera, *Iolanthe,* and a ballet, *Casse-Noisette,* Feb. Visit to Paris in a state of nervous depression, March. He conducts a Colonne concert, April 5. At Rouen he hears of the death of his sister, Alexandra Davidov. Arrival in New York, end of April. Concerts conducted in New York, Baltimore and Philadelphia, May. First performance of the symphonic ballad, *The Voyevoda* (Op. 78), at Siloti's (28) concert in Moscow, Nov. 18. New concert tour opens at Kiev, Dec.	
1892	52	Performance of *Eugene Oniegin,* rehearsed by Mahler (32), conducted by T. in Hamburg, Jan. 19. First performance of the *Casse-Noisette* Suite in St. Petersburg, March 19. After a visit to Vichy, T. sets to work on a symphony at his new country house at Klin, summer. Visits to Vienna, Salzburg and Prague. Production of *Iolanthe* and the *Casse-*	Honegger born, March 10; Lalo (69) dies, April 22; Milhaud born, Sept. 4.

Year	Age	Life	Contemporary Musicians

Noisette Ballet in St. Petersburg, Dec. 17. Concert conducted at Brussels. Dec. 29.

1893   53

After some performances conducted at Odessa, T. returns to Klin, Jan. He destroys last year's sketches for a Symphony and sets to work on the Symphony No. 6, B minor (Op. 74) ('Pathetic'), sketches a third piano Concerto (Op. 75) and writes 18 piano pieces (Op. 72). Philharmonic concert conducted in London, June 1. At Cambridge the musical doctor's degree is conferred on T., Boito (51), Bruch (55), Saint-Saëns (58) and Grieg (50), the last being absent. A concert of works by these composers and of Stanford (41) is performed, June 13. Return to Russia, end of June. Sixth Symphony performed in St. Petersburg under T.'s direction, Oct. 28. He feels slightly indisposed and at lunch drinks a glass of unboiled water.

Gounod (75) dies, Oct. 18. Akimenko aged 17; Albeniz 33; Alexandrov 5; Arensky 32; Balakirev 57; Bantock 25; Bartók 12; Bax 10; Berg 8; Bliss 2; Bloch, 13; Boito 51; Brahms 60; Bridge (Frank) 14; Bruch 55; Bruckner 69; Busoni 27; Casella 10; Catoire 32; Chabrier 52; Chausson 38; Cui 58; Debussy 31; Delius 31; Dohnányi 16; Dukas 28; Duparc 45; Dvořák 52; Elgar 36; Falla 17; Fauré 48; Feinberg 3; Glazunov 28; Glière 17; Gniessin 10; Goldmark 63; Granados 26; Grechaninov 29; Grieg 50; Holst 19; Honegger 1; Humperdinck 39; d'Indy 42; Ippolitov-Ivanov 34; Ireland 14; Janáček 39; Juon 21; Kalinnikov 27; Kastalsky 37; Kodály 11; Koreschenko 23; Krein (G.) 13; Krein (A.) 10; Leoncavallo 35; Liadov

Year	Age	Life	Contemporary Musicians
		Nov. **2.** He develops cholera. Tchaikovsky dies in St. Petersburg, Nov. **6.**	38; Liapunov 34; Mac-Dowell 32; Mackenzie 46; Mahler 33; Malipiero 11; Martucci 37; Massenet 51; Mascagni 30; Medtner 13; Miaskovsky 12; Milhaud 1; Novák 23; Parry 45; Pedrell 52; Pfitzner 24; Pizzetti 13; Prokofiev 2; Puccini 35; Rachmaninov 20; Ravel 18; Rebikov 27; Reger 20; Reinecke 69; Respighi 14; Rimsky-Korsakov 49; Roussel 24; Rubinstein (A.) 63; Saint-Saëns 58; Schmitt (Florent) 23; Schönberg 19; Scott (Cyril) 14; Scriabin 21; Sgambati 50; Sibelius 28; Sinding 37; Smyth (Ethel) 35; Sokolov 34; Stainer 53; Stanford 41; Strauss (J. ii) 68; Strauss (R.) 29; Stravinsky 11; Suk 19; Sullivan 51; Svendsen 53; Szymanow-ski 10; Taneiev 37; Tche-repnin (N.) 20; Thomas (A.) 82; Vassilenko 21; Vaughan Williams 21; Wolf 33.

APPENDIX B

CATALOGUE OF WORKS

DRAMATIC WORKS

(a) Operas

Opus

3. *The Voyevoda* (Ostrovsky). Extant: Overture and Entr'acte with Airs de Ballet.

Undine (Sollogoub-Shukovsky). Extant: Wedding March introduced as *andantino marziale* in second Symphony; aria used in *Snegourotchka*; *adagio* used in *The Swan Lake*.

Mandragora (Rachinsky). Unfinished. Extant: Piano version of *Chorus of Insects*, orchestrated by Glazounov.

The Oprichnik (Lashetchnikov). Earliest surviving opera.

14. *Vakula the Smith* (Gogol) (afterwards remodelled as *Tcherevichki*, or *Oxana's Caprices*).

24. *Eugene Oniegin* (Pushkin).

Joan of Arc (Schiller).

Mazeppa (Pushkin).

Oxana's Caprices. See above.

The Sorceress (Shpashinsky).

68. *The Queen of Spades* (Pushkin).

69. *Iolanthe* (Hendrik Herz).

(b) Incidental Music

12. *Snegourotchka* (Ostrovsky). Introduction, etc., soli and choruses.

The Voyevoda (Ostrovsky). One-scene manuscript.

67A. *Hamlet* (Shakespeare). Overture (abridged version of Op. 67) and 16 incidental numbers.

(c) Ballets

Opus

20. *The Swan Lake.*
66. *The Sleeping Beauty* (Perrault).
71. *Casse-Noisette* (Hoffmann).

ORCHESTRAL WORKS

(a) Symphonies

13. Symphony No. 1, G minor (*Winter Dreams*).
17. Symphony No. 2, C minor ('Little-Russian').
29. Symphony No. 3, D major ('Polish').
36. Symphony No. 4, F minor.
58. *Manfred.*
64. Symphony No. 5, E minor.
75 & 79. Symphony sketched but not completed. See under Piano Concertos.
74. Symphony No. 6, B minor ('Pathetic').

(b) Overtures, Fantasies, etc.

76. Overture, *The Storm* (Ostrovsky).
    Overture, C minor (unpublished).
15. Festival Overture on the Danish Hymn.
77. Symphonic Poem, *Fatum.*
    Fantasy-Overture, *Romeo and Juliet.*
18. Symphonic Fantasy, *The Tempest.*
32. Symphonic Fantasy, *Francesca da Rimini.*
49. Festival Overture, *The Year 1812.*
67. Fantasy-Overture, *Hamlet.* See also Incidental Music.
78. Symphonic Ballad, *The Voyevoda* (Pushkin).

Appendix B—Catalogue of Works

(c) Suites

Opus

43. Suite No. 1 (*Introduction and Fugue, Divertimento, Intermezzo, Marche militaire, Scherzo, Gavotte*).

53. Suite No. 2 (*Jeu de sons, Valse, Scherzo burlesque, Rêves d'enfant, Danse baroque, style Dargomizhsky*).

55. Suite No. 3 (*Élégie, Valse mélancolique, Scherzo, Theme and Variations*).

61. Suite No. 4, *Mozartiana* (*Gigue, Minuet, Preghiera, Theme and Variations*).

71A. Suite from *Casse-Noisette* Ballet.

(d) Miscellaneous

31. *Marche slave.*

45. *Capriccio italien.*

48. Serenade for string orchestra.

 Coronation March.

 Elegy for string orchestra (in memory of Samarin).

 Marche solennelle (for the Law Students).

 Marche militaire (for the band of the 98th regiment of Infantry).

(e) Concertos and Concert Pieces with Orchestra

23. Concerto No. 1, B flat minor, piano.

26. *Sérénade mélancolique,* violin.

33. *Variations on a Rococo Theme,* cello.

34. *Valse-Scherzo,* violin.

35. Concerto, D major, violin.

44. Concerto No. 2, G major, piano.

56. Concert Fantasy (*Quasi Rondo* and *Contrasts*), piano.

62. *Pezzo capriccioso,* cello.

Tchaikovsky

Opus

75. Concerto No. 3, E flat major (first movement adapted from discarded symphony), piano.
79. Andante and Finale (second and third movements adapted by Taneiev from same source), piano.

CHAMBER MUSIC

Sextet

70. *Souvenir de Florence,* for 2 violins, 2 violas, cello and double bass.

Quartets

11. String Quartet No. 1, D major.
22. String Quartet No. 2, F major.
30. String Quartet No. 3, E flat minor.

Trio

50. Trio, A minor, for piano, violin and cello.

Violin and Piano

42. *Souvenir d'un lieu cher.*   Three Pieces.
    Méditation ; Scherzo ; Mélodie.

PIANO MUSIC

Solo

Sonata, C sharp minor (posthumous).
1. Two Pieces.
   Scherzo à la russe ; Impromptu.

Appendix B—Catalogue of Works

Opus

2. *Souvenir de Hapsal.* Three Pieces.
   The Ruined Castle ; Scherzo ; Chant sans paroles.

4. *Valse-Caprice.*

5. *Romance,* F minor.

7. *Valse-Scherzo,* A major.

8. *Capriccio,* G flat major.

9. Three Pieces.
   Rêverie ; Polka de salon ; Mazurka de salon.

10. Two Pieces.
    Nocturne ; Humoresque.

19. Six Pieces.
    *Rêverie du soir ; Scherzo humoristique ; Feuillet d'album ;
    Nocturne ; Capriccioso ; Thème original et Variations.*

21. Six Pieces on one Theme.
    Prelude ; Fugue ; Impromptu ; Funeral March ; Mazurka ; Scherzo.

37. Sonata, G major.

37A. *The Seasons.* Twelve Characteristic Pieces.
    1. January: *At the Fireside.* 2. February: *Carnival.* 3. March:
    Song of the Lark. 4. April: *Snowdrop.* 5. May: *May-Night.*
    6. June: *Barcarolle.* 7. July: *Reaper's Song.* 8. August:
    Harvest. 9. September: *Hunting (The Chase).* 10. October:
    Autumn Song. 11. November: *Troika.* 12. December:
    Christmas.

39. Children's Album.
    1. *Morning Prayer.* 2. *Winter Morning.* 3. *The Little Horseman.*
    4. *Mamma.* 5. *March of Wooden Soldiers.* 6. *The Sick
    Doll.* 7. *Dollie's Funeral.* 8. *Valse.* 9. *The New Doll.*
    10. *Mazurka.* 11. *Russian Folksong.* 12. *The Peasant Preludes.*

Tchaikovsky

Opus

13. *Folk-song* (*Kamarinskaya*). 14. *Polka.* 15. *Italian Song.*
16. *Old French Melody.* 17. *German Song.* 18. *Neapolitan
Song.* 19. *The Old Nurse's Song.* 20. *The Witch.* 21. *Sweet
Dreams.* 22. *Song of the Lark.* 23. *Barrel-Organ.* 24. *In
Church.*

40. Twelve Pieces of Moderate Difficulty.

1. *Étude.* 2. *Chanson triste.* 3. *Funeral March.* 4. *Mazurka.*
5. *Mazurka.* 6. *Chant sans paroles.* 7. *In the Village.*
8. *Valse.* 9. *Valse.* 10. *Russian Dance.* 11. *Scherzo.*
12. *Rêverie interrompue.*

51. Six Pieces.

*Valse de salon ; Polka peu dansante ; Menuetto scherzoso ; Natha-
Valse ; Romance ; Valse sentimentale.*

Impromptu-Capriccio.

59. *Dumka.* Rustic Scene in Russia.

Valse-Scherzo, A major.

Impromptu.

72. Eighteen Pieces.

1. *Impromptu.* 2. *Berceuse.* 3. *Tendres reproches.* 4. *Danse
caractéristique.* 5. *Méditation.* 6. *Mazurka pour danser.*
7. *Polacca de concert.* 8. *Dialogue.* 9. *Un poco di Schumann.*
10. *Scherzo-Fantaisie.* 11. *Valse-Bluette.* 12. *L'Espiègle.*
13. *Écho rustique.* 14. *Chant élégiaque.* 15. *Un poco di
Chopin.* 16. *Valse à 5 temps.* 17. *Passé lointain.* 18. *Scène
dansante.*

Momento lirico. Impromptu. Unfinished. Completed by
Taneiev.

Duet

Fifty Russian Folksongs.

Appendix B—Catalogue of Works

VOCAL MUSIC

Songs [1]

6. Six Songs.

> 1. *Heed not!* (A. Tolstoy) (*F.W.*).   2. *A Summer Love Tale*
> (A. Pletcheyev) (*F.W.*).   3. *What torment, what rapture* (G.
> Rastopchin) (*N.M.*).   4. *A heavy tear* (A. Tolstoy) (*N.M.*).
> 5. *Warum?* (Heine) (*N.M.*).   6. *Nur wer die Sehnsucht kennt*
> (Goethe) (*N.M.*) (*F.W.*).

16. Six Songs.

> 1. *Berceuse* (Maikov).   2. *Attends!* (Grekov).   3. *This only
> once* (Maikov) (*N.M.*).   4. *The song that you sang long ago*
> (A. Pletcheyev) (*N.M.*).   5. *What matters?* (anon.) (*N.M.*).
> 6. *Chanson grecque* (Maikov).

25. Six Songs.

> 1. *The Sleep of Sorrow* (Stcherbina) (*N.M.*).   2. *Comme sur la
> cendre encore chaude* (Tiutchev).   3. *Kennst du das Land*
> (Goethe) (*N.M.*).   4. *Canary Bird* (Mey) (*N.M.*).   5. *Je ne
> lui ai jamais parlé* (Mey).   6. *The Tsar's Drinking House*
> (Mey) (*N.M.*).

27. Six Songs.

> 1. *Invocation to Sleep* (Ogarev) (*N.M.*).   2. *Clouds* (Grekov)
> (*F.W.*).   3. *O, never leave me, sweet friend* (Fet) (*N.M.*).
> 4. *Le Soir* (Mey, after Shevtchenko).   5. *Mother dear, oh,
> was I born* (Mey, after Mickiewicz) (*N.M.*).   6. *A Love
> Paean* (Mey, after Mieckiewicz) (*F.W.*).

---

[1] French translations of the titles are given from the complete
thematic catalogue of Tchaikovsky's works; German and Italian
titles only where they are original; where the songs are well known
under English titles, these are given from Lady Macfarren's collection
(Novello) and marked (N.M.) and from the selection translated by
F. J. Wishaw (Boosey), marked (F.W.).

Tchaikovsky

Opus

28. Six Songs.

    1. *No, whom I love I will not name* (Grekov, after Musset) (*N.M.*).
    2. *Les Corails* (Mey, after Syrokomlia). 3. *Why?* (Mey)
    (*N.M.*). 4. *No, I have never loved* (Apoutchin) (*N.M.*).
    5. *No tidings came from thee* (Tolstoy) (*N.M.*). 6. *Sweet
    maid, give answer* (anon.) (*N.M.*).

38. Six Songs.

    1. *Spanish Serenade* (*Don Juan's Serenade*) (A. Tolstoy) (*N.M.*)
    (*F.W.*). 2. *The Dawn of Spring* (A. Tolstoy) (*N.M.*).
    3. *The tapers were flashing* (A. Tolstoy) (*N.M.*). 4. *Oh,
    could you but for one short hour* (A. Tolstoy) (*N.M.*).
    5. *L'amour d'un mort* (Lermontov). 6. *'Non contrastar cogl'
    uomini'* (*Fifinella*) (Florentine folk poem) (*N.M.*) (*F.W.*).

47. Seven Songs.

    1. *Si je le savais* (A. Tolstoy). 2. *Unsatisfied* (A. Tolstoy)
    (*F.W.*). 3. *Le soir et le matin* (Mickiewicz). 4. *The sounds
    of day are still* (A. Tolstoy) (*F.W.*). 5. *To the Forest* (A.
    Tolstoy) (*F.W.*). 6. *Only for thee* (Apoutchin) (*F.W.*).
    7. *J'étais une petite herbe* (Sourikov).

54. Sixteen Songs for Children (Pletcheyev).

    1. *Grandmother and Grandson*. 2. *The Birdlet*. 3. *Spring*.
    4. *My Garden* (*F.W.*). 5. *Legend* ('*Christ in His Garden*')
    (*F.W.*). 6. *By the Strand*. 7. *Winter Evening*. 8. *The
    Cuckoo* (*F. W.*). 9. *Spring*. 10. *Cradle Song during a Storm*
    (*F.W.*). 11. *The Floweret*. 12. *Winter*. 13. *Spring Song*.
    14. *Autumn*. 15. *The Swallow*. 16. *Lullaby* (*F.W.*).

57. Six Songs (anon.).

    1. *Dis-moi, à quoi penses-tu?* 2. *Remorse* (*F.W.*). 3. *Ne me
    questionne pas*. 4. *Je voudrais m'endormir pour toujours*. 5. *Con-
    solation* (*F.W.*). 6. *Toi seul, tu croyais à mes souffrances*.

Appendix B—Catalogue of Works

Opus

60. Twelve Songs (anon.).

   1. *Absence* (*F.W.*). 2. *Je ne te dirai rien.* 3. *Ah! si vous saviez.* 4. *Le Rossignol.* 5. *Plain Words* (*F.W.*). 6. *Les Nuits sans sommeil.* 7. *La Chanson d'une Bohémienne.* 8. *Adieu.* 9. *La Nuit.* 10. *La Tête blanche.* 11. *Courage.* 12. *Nuit étoilée.*

63. Six Songs (anon.).

   1. *Do you remember?* (*F.W.*). 2. *New Hopes* (*F.W.*). 3. *You do not love me* (*F.W.*). 4. *Morning* (*F.W.*). 5. *A Night in July* (*F.W.*). 6. *A Serenade* (*F.W.*).

65. Six French Songs.

   1. *A Message* (E. Turquety) (*F.W.*). 2. *A Broken Tryst* (Paul Collin) (*F.W.*). 3. *Waiting* (Paul Collin) (*F.W.*). 4. *Let Winter come* (Paul Collin) (*F.W.*). 5. *Tears* (A. M. Blanchecotte) (*F.W.*). 6. *A Little Witch* (Paul Collin) (*F.W.*).

73. Six Songs (anon.).

   1. *An dem schlummernden Strom.* 2. *Nacht.* 3. *O du mondbelle Nacht.* 4. *Sonne ging zur Ruhe.* 5. *In trüber Stund.* 6. *Weil ich wie einstmals allein.*

   L'Oublié (Apoutchin).

   Emporte mon cœur (Fet).

   Des Frühlings blaue Augen (Heine).

   Je voudrais mettre dans une seule parole (Mey).

   Nous ne nous promènerons plus longtemps (Grekov).

Duets

46. Six Duets.

   1. *Le Soir* (J. Sourikov). 2. *Ballade écossaise* (A. Tolstoy). 3. *Larmes humaines* (Tiutchev). 4. *Au jardin, près de la rivière* (J. Sourikov). 5. *La Passion finie* (A. Tolstoy). 6. *L'Aube* (J. Sourikov).

   Romeo and Juliet, soprano and tenor.   Completed by Taneiev.

Tchaikovsky

Partsongs

Nature and Love, trio, 2 sopranos and contralto, with piano.
Night, quartet, S.A.T.B., with piano (after Mozart).

A Cappella

41. Liturgy of St. John Chrysostom (Russian Mass).
52. Russian Vesper Service.
    Nine Liturgical choruses.
    Hymn to SS. Cyril and Methodius.
    Homage to Anton Rubinstein.
    Chorus dedicated to choristers of Imperial Opera.
    Chorus for Students of Moscow University (male voices).

Cantatas

Schiller's *Ode to Joy* (manuscript).
Cantata for tenor solo, chorus and orchestra (manuscript).
Moscow Cantata, for solo voices, chorus and orchestra, for coronation
   of Alexander III.

ARRANGEMENTS

Rubinstein's overture, *Ivan the Terrible,* for piano duet.
Weber's *Perpetuum mobile,* for the left hand.
Recitatives to Mozart's *Marriage of Figaro.*

LITERARY WORKS

Treatise on Harmony.
Numerous critical articles.

APPENDIX C

PERSONALIA

Albrecht, Karl, a native of Breslau, for twelve years conductor at the Imperial Opera in St. Petersburg. Of his sons Constantine Carlovich Albrecht (born *c.* 1835) was a cellist and choirmaster who became inspector of the Moscow Conservatoire and Nicholas Rubinstein's 'right hand.' He married in 1862 the daughter of Langer, an eminent professor of the piano.

Arensky, Anton Stepanovich (1861–1906), Russian composer of the eclectic school, although for a time a pupil of Rimsky-Korsakov (q.v.). Appointed professor at the Moscow Conservatoire in 1882.

Artôt, Marguerite Joséphine Désirée Montagney (1835–1907), Belgian operatic mezzo-soprano singer, daughter of a professor of the horn at the Brussels Conservatoire, but born in Paris. Pupil of Pauline Viardot-Garcia (q.v.). First sang at concerts in Belgium, Holland and England, but joined the Paris Opéra in 1858. Later appeared in Italy, Germany and Russia. Married Padilla (q.v.) in 1869.

Auber, Daniel François Esprit (1782–1871), French composer, mainly of operas, including *La Muette de Portici (Masaniello), Fra Diavolo, Le Domino noir, La Part du diable (Carlo Broschi)* and *Le Cheval de bronze.*

Auer, Leopold (1845–1930), Hungarian violinist settled in Russia until the Revolution, when he went to the U.S.A. Pupil of Dont in Vienna and Joachim at Hanover, professor of the St. Petersburg Conservatoire from 1868. Teacher of many eminent violinists.

Balakirev, Mili Alexeievich (1836/7–1910), Russian composer of the nationalist school, founder of the 'Kutchka' group, mainly self-taught, but a great inspirer of others. The symphonic poem *Tamara* and the fantasy *Islamey* for piano are among his best works.

Belaiev, Mitrofan Petrovich (1836–1907), Russian timber merchant and great musical amateur, founder of a publishing firm for the propagation of Russian music in 1885.

Bessel, Vassili Vassilievich (1843–1907), Russian music publisher, fellow-student of Tchaikovsky in St. Petersburg, where he was a violinist in the orchestra of the Imperial Ballet and founded a publishing firm in 1869.

Boito, Arrigo (1842–1918), Italian poet, critic and composer, author of numerous librettos of Italian operas, including Verdi's *Othello* and *Falstaff*. Composer of the operas *Mefistofele* and *Nerone*.

Borodin, Alexander Porphirievich (1834–87), Russian nationalist composer and professor of chemistry, much influenced by Balakirev (q.v.) as a member of the 'Kutchka.' His chief works are the opera *Prince Igor* and three symphonies (one unfinished).

Brandukov, A., celebrated cellist. Studied at the Moscow Conservatoire. Travelled much as a virtuoso.

Brodsky, Adolf (1851–1929), Russian violinist, pupil of Hellmesberger in Vienna; successively conductor at Kiev, professor at the Leipzig Conservatoire, leader of the Hallé Orchestra in Manchester and principal of the Royal College of Music there.

Bruch, Max (1838–1920), German composer, professor of composition in Berlin, 1892–1910.

Bülow, Hans von (1830–94), German pianist and conductor, first husband of Cosima Wagner.

Cui, Cesar Antonovich (1835–1918), Russian composer, critic and professor of fortifications, of French descent and born in Poland. Studying military engineering in St. Petersburg, he joined the 'Kutchka,' but supported its ideals by his writings rather than by his compositions, which are less nationalistic than those of the rest of the group.

Durgomizhsky, Alexander Sergeievich (1813–69), Russian composer who shares with Glinka (q.v.) the distinction of having founded a nationalist school. He had next to no professional training. His chief works are the operas *Roussalka* and *The Stone Guest,* the latter, on the subject of Don Juan, containing anticipations of devices used as 'modernisms' by later Russian and French composers.

Erdmannsdoerffer, Max (1848–1905), German conductor and composer, became in 1882 director of the Imperial Russian Musical Society at Moscow.

Fitzenhagen, Wilhelm Karl Friedrich (1848–90), German cellist, leader of the Imperial Russian Music Society at Moscow and professor at the Conservatoire.

Glazunov, Alexander, Constantinovich (born 1865), Russian composer, pupil of Rimsky-Korsakov (q.v.) and at first attached to the nationalist group, though not a member of the 'Kutchka'; became more and more eclectic and professional later. Appointed professor at the St. Petersburg Conservatoire in 1900 and director in 1906. His works include eight symphonies.

Glinka, Michael Ivanovich (1803–57), composer, often called 'the father of Russian music,' brought up musically in a half amateurish way until he studied under Dehn at Berlin in 1833. His first opera, *A Life for the Tsar,* is the beginning of national opera in Russia, and the second, *Russlan and Ludmilla,* contains many musical innovations.

Halit, Karl (1859–1909), Czech violinist, educated at the Prague Conservatoire and under Joachim, of whose quartet he became a member, besides leading one of his own.

Hanslick, Eduard (1825–1904), music critic in Vienna, lecturer on musical history.

Henschel, Isidor Georg (afterwards *Sir George*) (1850–1934), German singer, composer and conductor long settled in England and naturalized.

Hrimaly, Ivan, violinist at Moscow.

Hubert, Nicholas Albertovich (1840–88), son of a Russian teacher of the piano and fellow-pupil with Tchaikovsky at the St. Petersburg Conservatoire, became professor of theory at Moscow Conservatoire and succeeded Nicholas Rubinstein as head of that institution.

Juon, Paul (born 1872), Russian composer, pupil of Arensky (q.v.) and Taneiev (q.v.), settled in Berlin as professor of composition from 1897.

Jurgenson, Peter Ivanovich (born 1836), served first as salesman, then as manager, in various music-publishing firms in St. Petersburg and Moscow. On the last of these, that of the brothers Schildbach in Moscow, being dissolved, Jurgenson founded in 1861 the firm which bore his name until nationalized under the Revolution. It was for many years the leading music-publishing house in Russia, and issued nearly all Tchaikovsky's works.

Kashkin, Nicholas Dmitrievich (1839–c. 1909), Russian music critic and teacher, professor at the Moscow Conservatoire from its foundation in 1864 to 1896. Critic of the *Russky Viedomosti* and author of a volume of reminiscences of Tchaikovsky.

Klindworth, Karl (1830–1916), German pianist and conductor, pupil of Liszt and arranger of music for his instrument, including vocal scores of Wagner's work. He had a school of music of his own in Berlin.

Knorr, Ivan (1853–1916), Russo-German composer and teacher, student at the Leipzig Conservatoire, professor at Kharkov from 1874 and at Frankfort o/M. from 1883, where he became director of Hoch's Conservatoire in 1908.

Lamperti, Francesco (1813–92), Italian teacher of singing, master of many eminent vocalists and author of vocal studies and a treatise on singing.

Laroche, Herman Augustovich (1845–1904), Russian music critic, fellow-student of Tchaikovsky at the St. Petersburg Conservatoire, professor of the Moscow Conservatoire from 1867. Returned to

St. Petersburg in 1871. Critic of many leading Russian news-papers.

Laub, Ferdinand (1832–75), Czech violinist, studied at the Prague Conservatoire, and in Vienna from 1847. Travelled much and succeeded Joachim as leader of the court orchestra at Weimar in 1853. After a professorship at Stern's Conservatoire in Berlin, he was appointed chief violin professor at the Moscow Conservatoire in 1866.

Litolff, Henry Charles (1818–91), composer, pianist and music publisher born in England of an Alsatian father and an English mother. Appeared as a child pianist and travelled much, took over a music-publishing firm at Brunswick in 1851 and composed a large number of miscellaneous works.

Marmontel, Antoine François (1816–98), French pianist, teacher and musical scholar.

Mussorgsky, Modest Petrovich (1839–81), Russian nationalist composer, studied in an amateurish way and was introduced to Balakirev (q.v.) in 1857, joining the 'Kutchka' and developing a realistic art on the basis of national Russian music. The opera, *Boris Godunov*, is his masterpiece, but many of his smaller works, especially his remarkable songs, are better known in western Europe than his second full-size opera, *Khovanshtchina*.

Napravnik, Eduard (1839–1915), composer and conductor of the Russian school of Czech birth, student and teacher at the organ school in Prague. Went to Russia in 1861 and became first conductor of the court opera in 1869. He wrote four operas and numerous miscellaneous works.

Ostrovsky, Alexander Nicolaievich (1823–86), Russian dramatist, first practised as a lawyer and later became famous as author of many historical and sociological dramas.

Pabst, Paul (1854–97), German pianist, pupil of Liszt, teacher at the Moscow Conservatoire and author of numerous popular paraphrases.

Padilla y Ramos, Mariano (1842–1906) Spanish baritone singer, studied in Italy and toured Europe extensively. Married Désirée Artôt (q.v.) in 1869.

Petipa, Marius (1819–1910), dancer and choreographer, born at Marseilles, made his first appearance at Rachel's benefit with Carlotta Grisi at the Comédie-Française. Went to St. Petersburg in 1847 and became ballet-master at the Maryinski Theatre.

Rimsky-Korsakov, Nicholas Andreievich (1844–1908), Russian composer who began his career in the navy, but took to music after meeting Balakirev (q.v.), whose 'Kutchka' he joined. Became professor of orchestration at the St. Petersburg Conservatoire in 1871 and took a more academic view of his art than the rest of the nationalist group. His chief works are thirteen operas and several orchestral compositions.

Rubinstein, Anton (1830–94), Russian pianist and composer, made public appearances from his ninth year and became one of the greatest pianists of his day. As a composer, although immensely prolific, he is now almost entirely forgotten. The 'Ocean' Symphony and the opera, *The Demon*, were among his most successful works. He founded the St. Petersburg Conservatoire in 1862.

Rubinstein, Nicholas (1835–81), Russian pianist, conductor and composer, brother of the preceding. Studied in Berlin, founded the Russian Musical Society at Moscow in 1859 and the Conservatoire in 1866.

Serov, Alexander Nicolaievich (1820–71), Russian composer and critic; studied law, but found time to cultivate music, which eventually, after a career as civil servant, he succeeded in taking up professionally. The opera, *Judith*, is his best-known work.

Siloti, Alexander (born 1863), Russian pianist, student at the Moscow Conservatoire, 1875–81, and pupil of Liszt, 1883–6. Made extensive tours and became professor at the Moscow Conservatoire in 1890.

Smyth, Ethel Mary (born 1858), English composer and author, studied at Leipzig, where she produced several works. Her Mass was produced in London in 1893, and she has written a number of extensive works, including the operas, *The Wreckers* and *The Boatswain's Mate*, a cantata, *The Prison*, etc. She has published several books of reminiscences and is a Doctor of Music as well as a Dame of the British Empire.

Stassov, Vladimir Vassilievich (1824–1906), Russian critic and champion of the nationalist school represented by the 'Kutchka.'

Taneiev, Serge Ivanovich (1856–1915), Russian pianist and composer, student at the Moscow Conservatoire, where Tchaikovsky was his master of composition and succeeded him as professor on his retirement in 1878. His most important works, of a certain academic solidity, are orchestral and chamber music.

Viardot-Garcia, Pauline Michelle (1821–1910), Franco-Spanish soprano singer.

Zaremba, Nicholas Ivanovich (1824–79), professor of theory at St. Petersburg Conservatoire from its foundation in 1861. Succeeded Anton Rubinstein as director from 1867 to 1871. Was a pupil of A. B. Marx and remained under the influence of his German studies. Is lampooned in Moussorgsky's *Peepshow*.

APPENDIX D

BIBLIOGRAPHY [1]

Blom, Eric, 'Tchaikovsky's Orchestral Works.' ('Musical Pilgrim' Series; Oxford and London, 1927.)

Bowen, Catherine Drinker, and Meck, Barbara von, 'Beloved Friend: the Story of Tchaikovsky and Nadezhda von Meck.' (London, 1937.)

Huneker, James G., 'Mezzotints in Modern Music.' (London, 1899.)
—— 'Old Fogy. His Musical Opinions and Grotesques.' (New York, 1913.)

Knorr, Ivan, 'Tschaikowski' (in German). (Berlin, 1900.)

Lee, E. Markham, 'Tchaikovsky.' (Bell's Miniature Series; London, 1906.)
—— 'Tchaikovsky.' ('Music of the Masters' Series; London, 1906.)

Mann, Klaus, 'Pathetic Symphony.' A Novel. Translated by Hermon Ould. (London, 1938.)

Mason, Daniel Gregory, 'From Grieg to Brahms.' (London, 1902.)

Newmarch, Rosa, 'The Russian Opera.' (London, 1912.)
—— 'Tchaikovsky, his Life and Works.' (London, 1900.)

Pals, Nikolai von, 'Peter Tschaikowsky' (in German). (Potsdam, 1939.)

Stein, Richard H., 'Tschaikowskij' (in German). (Stuttgart, 1928.)

Tchaikovsky, Modest, 'The Life of Peter Ilyich Tchaikovsky.' Edited and abridged from the Russian and German editions by Rosa Newmarch. (London and New York, 1906.)

Weingartner, Felix, 'Symphony Writers since Beethoven.' Translated by A. Bles. (London, 1904.)

---

[1] The vast bibliography of works in Russian is excluded here as not likely to be of use to many readers of this book.

INDEX

ALBRECHT, Constantine Carlovich, 16, 159, 221
Albrecht, Karl, 221
Alexandra, Queen, 20
Andante cantabile. See Quartet No. 1
Arensky, 58, 152, 177, 221
Artôt, Désirée, 26–31, 46, 221
Assière, André, 2
Assière, Catherine, 2
Assière, Michael, 2
Auber, 27, 66, 221
Auer, Leopold, 166, 167, 221
Aurora's Wedding. See *Sleeping Beauty*

Bach, 17, 54
Backhaus, Wilhelm, 173
Bakst, Leon, 98
Balakirev, 22–6, 31, 33, 34, 59, 119, 124, 128, 129, 136, 137, 148, 222
Barbier, Jules, 75
Battle of Poltava, The, 82, 181
Beecham, Thomas, 104
Beethoven, 8, 9, 11, 16, 35, 83, 118, 122, 151
Begitchev, V. P., 94
Belaiev, M. P., 129, 135, 222

Berezovsky, 73, 80, 111
Berger, Francesco, 49
Berlioz, 10, 22, 123, 124, 137
Bessel, Vassili, 31, 173, 222
Bizet, 36, 41
Boito, Arrigo, 52, 222
Borodin, 22, 31, 33, 49, 59, 222
Bote & Bock, 32
Brahms, 42, 46, 47, 49, 177
Brandukov, A., 168, 222
Brodsky, Adolf, 46, 48, 167, 222
Bruch, Max, 52, 222
Bülow, Hans von, 144, 159, 162, 222
Busoni, 46

Capriccio italien, 146, 184
Casse-Noisette, ballet, 90, 99–103, 180, 181, 183
Chant sans paroles, for piano, 22, 171
Chorus of Insects, 59
Concert Fantasy. See Fantasy
Concertos, 159–68
  B flat minor, for piano (Op. 23), 35, 159–64
  D major, for violin (Op. 35), 166, 167

229

Concertos—*continued*
  E flat major, for piano (Op. 75), 165, 166
  G major, for piano (Op. 44), 164, 165
Coronation March, 147
Cui, 12, 22, 23, 25, 33, 61, 66, 80, 82, 222

Dagmar, Princess, of Denmark, 20
Dannreuther, Edward, 105
Dante, 132, 137
Dargomizhsky, 25, 59, 143, 223
Davidov, Alexandra, 12, 22, 27, 51
Davidov, Elizabeth, 19
Davidov, Mme, 19
Davidov, Vera, 19
Davidov, Vladimir, 99, 121
Debussy, 38
Delibes, 36, 41
Delius, 46
Dershavin, 89
Diaghilev, Serge, 98
Dumas, 99
Durbach, Fanny, 2, 3
Dvořák, 49

Elegy for orchestra, 149
Elgar, 145
Erdmannsdoerffer, Max, 144, 223
Eugene Oniegin, opera, 38, 39, 55, 68–75, 86, 90, 91, 184

Fantasy for piano and orchestra (Op. 56), 166
Fatum, fantasy for orchestra, 27, 31, 33, 128, 129, 180
Fitzenhagen, Wilhelm, 156, 168, 223
Francesca da Rimini, symphonic fantasy, 124, 131–3, 136, 137, 181, 183

Givochini, 27
Glazunov, 53, 122, 167, 223
Glinka, 9, 13, 22, 174, 223
Godfrey, Dan, 104, 179
Gogol, 61, 62
Grétry, 90
Grieg, 46–8, 52, 133

Halíř, Karl, 49, 223
Hamlet, fantasy-overture, 96, 133
Hamlet, incidental music, 95, 96, 133
Hanslick, Eduard, 176, 223
Helena, Grand Duchess, 61, 62
Henschel, George, 52, 223
Herz, Hendrik, 90
Hoffmann, E. T. A., 99
Hrimaly, Ivan, 154, 156, 223
Hubert, Nicholas, 17, 160, 161, 224
Huneker, James, 122

Iolanthe, opera, 90, 91, 99

Index

Jahn, Otto, 44
Joan of Arc, opera, 75–82, 91
Juon, Paul, vii, 184, 224
Jurgenson, Peter Ivanovich, 16, 17, 73, 81, 141, 147, 156, 171, 173–5, 224

Kadmina, actress, 94, 95
Kashkin, Nicholas, 17, 41, 59, 93, 107, 173, 224
Keeton, A. E., 30
Kindinger, Rudolf, 8
Klindworth, Karl, 162, 170, 224
Knorr, Ivan, 84, 108, 112, 131, 150, 224

Lamperti, Francesco, 26, 224
Laroche, Hermann, 9–13, 16–18, 57, 118, 128, 172, 224
Laub, Ferdinand, 154, 225
Lavrovskaya, Elizabeth, 38, 67
Liszt, 10, 16, 23, 36, 133
Litolff, Henry, 11, 23, 225
Little Shoes, The. See *Vakula the Smith*
Lvov, 58

Macfarren, Natalie, 177
Mandragora, unfinished opera, 35, 59
Manfred, symphony, 34, 44, 105, 123–7, 136, 180, 183
Manns, August, 111
Marche slave, 147
Marches, 146, 147

Marmontel, A. F., 38, 175, 225
Marx, theorist, 9
Mazeppa, opera, 80–3, 91, 181
Meck, Nadezhda von, 22, 37, 38, 41, 50, 51, 73, 112, 113, 159
Meck, Nicholas von, 51
Mendelssohn, 9, 17
Mermet, Auguste, 75
Meyerbeer, 79
Military March, 147
Milyukov, Antonina Ivanovna, 39. *See also* Tchaikovsky
Mozart, 3, 10, 44, 90, 91, 144–6, 151
Mozartiana. See Suite No. 4
Mussorgsky, 22, 33, 80, 225

Napravnik, Eduard, 79, 85, 123, 225
Nature and Love, vocal trio, 178
Newmarch, Rosa, vii, 41, 44, 68, 98, 105, 140, 184, 185
Nikisch, Arthur, 181
Nikulina, actress, 94
'Nur wer die Sehnsucht kennt, song, 49, 177
Nutcracker, The. See *Casse-Noisette*

Ode to Joy (Schiller), 12, 23
Oprichnik, The, opera, 35, 58–61, 65–7
Ostrovsky, A. N., 10, 27, 57–9, 93–5, 138, 225

Overtures:
  C minor, 18, 138
  F major, 12, 18, 138
  On the Danish National Hymn, 20, 138, 139
  The Storm, 10, 138, 180
  The Year 1812, 20, 139, 140, 181-3
Oxana's Caprices. See *Vakula the Smith*

Pabst, Paul, 184, 225
Padilla, Mariano, 31, 226
Paltchikov, Marie Markovna, 3
Peasant Girls' Dances, 12
Perrault, 98
Petipa, Marius, 101, 226
Pezzo capriccioso for cello and orchestra, 168
Philipov, piano teacher, 4
Piano music, 22, 169-77
Polonsky, 61
Pushkin, 38, 68, 82, 83, 85, 88-90, 133

Quartets for strings, 150-4
  No. 1, D major (Op. 11), 35, 151-3
  No. 2, F major (Op. 22), 152, 153
  No. 3, E flat minor (Op. 30), 153, 154
  B flat major (unfinished), 12, 150, 171

Queen of Spades, The, opera, 85-91

Richter, Hans, 180
Riemann, Hugo, 122
Rimsky-Korsakov, 22, 24-6, 31-4, 49, 66, 83, 119, 123, 140, 226
Romeo and Juliet, fantasy-overture, 31-3, 53, 124, 129-32, 137, 181, 184
Rossini, 66
Rubinstein, Anton, 9-12, 14, 15, 18-20, 22, 27, 28, 31, 74, 75, 138, 152, 173, 175, 226
Rubinstein, Nicholas, 14-18, 28, 32, 34-6, 41, 43, 60, 65, 74, 95, 107, 118, 128, 129, 142, 151, 152, 155-7, 159-62, 165, 170, 171, 226

Sadovsky, 27
Saint-Saëns, 36, 52
Samarin, actor, 94, 95, 149
Schiller, 12, 75
Schroeder, 49
Schubert, 11, 17, 177
Schumann, 8, 11, 16, 23, 127, 152, 172
Seasons, The, piano pieces, 173-4
Serenade for strings, 50, 147-9
Sérénade mélancolique for violin and orchestra, 167, 168
Serov, Alexander, 11, 12, 14, 61, 91, 226

Index

Sextet. See *Souvenir de Florence*

Shakespeare, 69, 133, 137

Shilovsky, Vladimir, 26, 35, 36, 38, 39, 68, 72

Shpashinsky, 84

Siloti, Alexander, 46, 49, 134, 135, 226

Skobelev, general, 147

Sleeping Beauty, The, ballet, 98, 101

Smyth, Ethel, 48, 49, 226

Snegourochka, incidental music, 58, 93–5, 157

Sofronov, servant, 43

Sologub, Count, 58

Sonatas for piano:
  C sharp minor (posthumous), 170
  G major (Op. 37), 170

Songs, 84, 152, 177–8

Sorceress, The, opera, 84, 85–91

Souvenir de Florence, sextet for strings, 85, 150, 155

Spitta, Philipp, 54

Stassov, Vladimir, 25, 33, 227

Strauss, Johann, 12

Strauss, Richard, 121

Suites for orchestra, 140–6
  No. 1 (Op. 43), 49, 141, 142
  No. 2 (Op. 53), 142, 143
  No. 3 (Op. 55), 50, 143–5, 180–2
  No. 4 (*Mozartiana*, Op. 61), 144–6, 181

Swan Lake, The, ballet, 38, 58, 96–8

Symphonies, 53, 104–27, 179–81
  No. 1, G minor (*Winter Dreams*, Op. 13), 19, 20, 24, 26, 105–7, 170
  No. 2, C minor ('Little Russian,' Op. 17), 58, 107–112, 149, 173, 184
  No. 3, D major ('Polish,' Op. 29), 111, 112
  No. 4, F minor (Op. 36), 38, 52, 104, 112–20, 123, 181
  No. 5, E minor (Op. 64), 104, 112, 120, 121, 123, 181
  No. 6, B minor ('Pathetic,' Op. 74), 6, 52, 104, 112, 120–3, 181, 183, 184

Taneiev, 74, 117, 135, 142, 156, 164–6, 177, 227

Tchaikovsky, Alexandra Andreievna (mother), 2, 5, 6

Tchaikovsky, Alexandra Ilyovna (sister), 2. *See also* Davidov

Tchaikovsky, Anatol Ilyich (brother), 4, 18, 30, 80, 164

Tchaikovsky, Andrei Petrovich (cousin), 147

Tchaikovsky, Antonina Ivanovna (wife), 39–41

Tchaikovsky, Feodor Afanassievich (great-grandfather), 1

Tchaikovsky, Hippolytus Ilyich (brother), 2

233

Tchaikovsky, Ilya Petrovich (father), 1–8, 27–9, 39, 60
Tchaikovsky, Lydia Vladimirovna (cousin), 2, 3
Tchaikovsky, Maria Karlovna (father's first wife), 2
Tchaikovsky, Modest Ilyich (brother), vii, 4, 18, 21, 23, 27, 36, 37, 49, 52, 58, 60, 67, 76, 85, 90, 101, 164, 184
Tchaikovsky, Nicholas Ilyich (brother), 2, 4, 9
Tchaikovsky, Peter Feodorovich (grandfather), 1
Tchaikovsky, Peter Petrovich (uncle), 6
Tcherevichki. See *Vakula the Smith*
Tempest, The, orchestral fantasy, 33, 131, 137
Trio, A minor, for violin, cello and piano, 43, 95, 155–8
Turgenev, 35

Undine, opera, 31, 32, 35, 58, 59, 108

Vacker, M. A., 5
Vakula the Smith, opera, 62–7, 83
Valse-Scherzo for violin and orchestra, 168
Variations on a Rococo Theme for cello and orchestra, 168
Verdi, 80, 91
Viardot-Garcia, Pauline, 26, 227
Voyevoda Dances, 21, 23–5
Voyevoda, The, incidental music, 95, 180
Voyevoda, The, opera, 12, 21, 22, 26, 31, 57–9
Voyevoda, The, symphonic ballad, 133–5

Wagner, 10, 11, 16, 23, 36, 42, 91
Wallon, Henri, 75
Walzeck, Mme, 178
Wood, Henry J., 82, 104, 180–2

Zaremba, Nicholas, 9, 19, 227
Zhukovsky, 58, 75